200 super salads

D0381894

hamlyn | all colour cookbook

200 super salads

Alice Storey

An Hachette UK company
www.hachette.co.uk

First published in Great Britain in 2009 by Hamlyn,
a division of Octopus Publishing Group Ltd
2–4 Heron Quays, London E14 4JP
www.octopusbooks.co.uk

ISBN: 978-0-600-61901-7

A CIP catalogue record for this book is available
from the British Library

Printed and bound in China

1 2 3 4 5 6 7 8 9 10

Both metric and imperial measurements are given for the
recipes. Use one set of measures only, not a mixture of both.

Standard level spoon measurements are used in all recipes
1 tablespoon = 15 ml
1 teaspoon = 5 ml

Ovens should be preheated to the specified temperature.
If using a fan-assisted oven, follow the manufacturer's
instructions for adjusting the time and temperature.

The varieties of cheese used in this book may not always
be strictly vegetarian, but many cheeses are available in
vegetarian form. Always check the label so that you know
what you are buying.

Eggs should be medium unless otherwise stated;
choose free-range if possible and preferably organic. The
Department of Health advises that eggs should not be
consumed raw. This book contains some dishes made with
raw or lightly cooked eggs. It is prudent for more vulnerable
people, such as pregnant and nursing mothers, invalids, the
elderly, babies and young children, to avoid uncooked or
lightly cooked dishes made with eggs.

This book includes dishes made with nuts and nut
derivatives. It is advisable for those with known allergic
reactions to nuts and nut derivatives and those who may
be potentially vulnerable to these allergies, such as pregnant
and nursing mothers, invalids, the elderly, babies and
children, to avoid dishes made with nuts and nut oils. It is
also prudent to check the labels of preprepared ingredients
for the possible inclusion of nut derivatives.

contents

introduction

introduction

A salad can be a simple side dish, served to complement a main course of meat or fish, or it can be a meal in itself, whether it is a light lunch or quickly prepared evening meal, or as an impressive and filling main course for a dinner party.

Salads are created from a combination of foods that are limited only by the imagination. The range and variety of salads that can be made are as diverse as the cultures from which they come, whether it is a hearty, mayonnaise-based potato salad or japanese beef & noodle salad. All salads are best made with seasonally available ingredients, and the recipes should, therefore, be adjusted according to the time of year, to what looks best and to what is readily obtainable in the shops and in your garden.

Salad leaves
There is such a variety of ingredients readily available from countries all over the world that it is possible to experiment with different combinations and to use ingredients that are unusual and exciting. Even the smallest supermarket offers an extraordinary range of lettuces and salad mixes, from common iceberg and cos lettuces, to baby spinach mix, beetroot mix, baby leaf and herbs, radicchio, rocket and watercress to lamb's lettuce, and if you look in more specialist shops you might find dandelion leaves, chicory, tatsoi, tarvido, sorrel and many more. Even edible flowers, such as nasturtiums and marigolds, make a pretty addition to salads. You can also easily grow a range of cut-and-come again salad leaves in even the smallest garden, and it's possible to buy seeds of unusual cabbages and lettuces that are quick to cultivate.

Dressings
Not only can the ingredients in a salad be adapted according to what is available but the range of dressings used to accompany them is almost endless. Overall a salad dressing not only lubricates the salad but also makes it more flavourful and pleasant to eat. Probably the simplest dressing for a salad is vinaigrette, which, at its most basic, is a simple combination of one part acid to three

parts oil. The ingredients can be emulsified to make a smooth paste or simply shaken so that they are loosely combined, resulting in a broken vinaigrette. An emulsion is the blending of two unmixable ingredients, and the mixture is stabilized by the addition to mayonnaise of egg yolks, which contain lecithin, or one of the many types of mustard that are now available.

A basic recipe for vinaigrette is given on page 13, but because there are so many wonderful vinegars available you can adapt the recipe to suit the ingredients in the salad and your own personal preferences. Look out for cabernet sauvignon, chardonnay, balsamic, aceto balsamico, white balsamic, rice wine, cider, red and black Chinese and sherry vinegars, as well as vinegars flavoured with different herbs and fruits.

Using the best quality vinegar and oil are extremely important when it comes to making a good salad into a great one, and when you are simply drizzling olive oil over salads, particularly ones that contain tomatoes, use the finest extra virgin olive oil you can find. However, when you are making a vinaigrette you might prefer to use a less strongly flavoured, light olive oil, because the strong flavour of extra virgin olive oil can overwhelm the other, less dominant ingredients. If you make a vinaigrette it will keep for a few days in the refrigerator but remember to shake it vigorously before using so that the oil and vinegar recombine.

It is possible to flavour fairly neutral vinegars, such as white wine vinegar, by adding herbs and spices, including tarragon (see page 14), chilli and rosemary. Many vinaigrette recipes incorporate fruit and vegetables, such as olives (see page 13), orange, lime, lemon, pomegranate, tomatoes and clementines. Fruit juice is a wonderful supplement for vinegar as long as the sugar in the fruit complements the ingredients of the salad. The acid from both the fruit juice and the vinegar can be useful for making the raw onion that is often included in salads more digestible. If you mix raw onion into the dressing 15 minutes before adding the dressing to the salad the onion will lose its harshness but retain its flavour.

Although vinaigrette dressings are usually quick to make and light and healthy, there are many other wonderful dressings for salads, including richer ones based on creamy cheeses and mayonnaise. Like vinaigrette, mayonnaise is an emulsion, but it contains egg yolks as well as oil and vinegar and, if liked, mustard of some kind. A basic recipe is given on page 12. Mayonnaise is a great base and can be flavoured with all types of ingredients, including seeded mustards, capers, lemon, anchovies, horseradish, garlic (when it becomes Aïoli; see page 12), herbs and cheese. Mayonnaise-based dressings go particularly well with seafood, but they can be adapted to almost any salad, and many of the dressings used with potato salads are based on mayonnaise, including some of the best known ready-made versions, such as Thousand Island Dressing and Ranch Dressing.

Among the other popular creamy dressings are those based on blue cheese (see page 14), but you can adapt the recipe to incorporate other soft cheeses, including goats' cheese, according to the ingredients in the salad. Creamy dressings are the perfect accompaniment for classic combinations such

as apples and pears, when the fruits cut through the richness of the dressing and provide a pleasant counterbalance.

Another way to add interesting flavours to dressings is to use one of the different flavoured oils that are now available. Among the flavoured oils that you can choose from are walnut, hazelnut, chilli, garlic, lemon and herb. It is also easy to make your own flavoured oils (see page 15).

Grains, pasta & pulses
Grains and pulses are a useful addition to salads, transforming them into filling and satisfying meals, and among the interesting pulses and grains you can try are buckwheat, wild rice, kidney beans, cannellini beans, butter beans, chickpeas, couscous and quinoa. Canned beans are particularly useful, needing neither the lengthy soaking nor the cooking of the dried types.

Pasta and noodles are also useful for adding bulk and a change of texture to a salad. There is a huge range to choose from, and you can enhance your salads with Italian pastas, such as orecchiette, orzo and penne, or Asian noodles, including vermicelli noodles, rice noodles, egg noodles, soba noodles and cellophane noodles. Pasta and noodle salads are delicious served both warm and cold, and they make healthy and satisfying meals. For extra crunch you can add croûtons to salads. These are now available ready made, but they are quick and easy to make (see page 44). You can use any type of bread you like and flavour it with herbs, different oils, garlic and cheese. Vary the size of the croûtons according to your own preference and the other ingredients of the salad.

Fruit

Fruit salads are, of course, among the most popular and easy to prepare of all desserts, but fruit can be used in savoury salads too, providing a welcome – and sometimes unexpected – contrast of flavours and textures. Pears and Parmesan cheese are a classic combination, but other fruits are ideal accompaniments for meat and cheese.

A salad of fresh fruits is usually a refreshing and palate-cleansing end to a meal, especially if the preceding courses have been rich and heavy, but fruit salads can be special with the combination of exotic fruit and unusual flavours, such as black pepper, basil, tarragon, rosewater and balsamic vinegar. Enhance simple fruit salads by the addition of nuts, mascarpone cheese, crème fraîche, yogurt, whipped cream, ice cream, custard, ginger biscuits, chocolate, amaretti biscuits and even alcohol.

Salads no longer have to be viewed as the 'healthy' option when it comes to planning meals. The recipes that follow suggest some interesting combinations or ingredients, textures and flavours to whet your appetite and show that a salad can be a regular addition to your menu.

basic recipes

mayonnaise

Serves 6–8
Preparation time 10 minutes

2 egg yolks
2 teaspoons **Dijon mustard**
1–2 tablespoons **white wine vinegar**
250 ml (8 fl oz) **olive oil**
salt and **pepper**

Put the egg yolks, mustard, 1 tablespoon
vinegar and a little salt and pepper into a
large bowl and whisk lightly with a balloon
whisk to combine. Whisking continuously,
start adding the olive oil, a few drops at a
time, until the sauce starts to thicken.
Gradually add the remaining oil in a very thin,
steady stream until the mayonnaise is thick
and glossy. Don't add the oil too quickly or the
mayonnaise might start to separate. If this
happens, try whisking in 1 tablespoon warm
water. If the mixture curdles completely, whisk
another egg yolk in a separate bowl and
gradually whisk it into the curdled sauce.
Check the seasoning, adding a little more
vinegar if the sauce tastes bland. Mayonnaise
can be kept, covered, in the refrigerator for
up to 2 days.

aïoli

Serves 6–8
Preparation time 10 minutes

2 egg yolks
1 teaspoon **Dijon mustard**
1–2 tablespoons **lemon juice**
2 **garlic cloves**, crushed
good pinch of **cayenne pepper**
250 ml (8 fl oz) **sunflower oil** or **olive oil**
salt

Put the egg yolks, mustard, 1 tablespoon
lemon juice, the garlic, cayenne pepper and
a little oil in a large bowl and whisk together
lightly to combine. Follow the Mayonnaise
recipe (see above) from the second step.
Cover and chill until ready to serve.

vinaigrette

Serves 4
Preparation time 10 minutes

1 teaspoon **caster sugar**
pinch of **dry mustard**
2 tablespoons **wine vinegar**
4–6 tablespoons **olive oil**
salt and **pepper**

Whisk together the sugar and mustard with
the vinegar. Add the oil, season to taste with
salt and pepper and mix together thoroughly.
Alternatively, put the ingredients in a screw-
top jar, replace the lid and shake well.

olive vinaigrette

Serves 4
Preparation time 10 minutes

1 **garlic clove**
1–2 pitted **black olives**
2 tablespoons **balsamic vinegar**
2 tablespoons **lime juice**
1 tablespoon **Dijon mustard**

Crush the garlic and finely chop the olives.
Whisk them with the vinegar, lime juice and
mustard. Alternatively, put the ingredients in

a screw-top jar, replace the lid and shake well
to combine.

low-calorie french dressing

Serves 8
Preparation time 10 minutes

½ small **onion**
6 tablespoons **olive oil**
2 tablespoons **wine vinegar**
½ teaspoon **mustard**
½ tablespoon **caster sugar**
pinch of **ground coriander**
3 tablespoons chopped **parsley**
salt and **pepper**

Grate the onion. Whisk together all the
ingredients until thickened. Season to taste
with salt and pepper. Alternatively, put the
ingredients, including the grated onion, in a
screw-top jar, replace the lid and shake well.

blue cheese dressing

Serves 4
Preparation time 10 minutes

1 teaspoon **caster sugar**
pinch of **dry mustard**
2 tablespoons **wine vinegar**
4–6 tablespoons **olive oil**
25 g (1 oz) **blue cheese**, such as **Roquefort**
salt and **pepper**

Whisk together the sugar and mustard with
the vinegar. Add the oil and the crumbled
cheese, season to taste with salt and pepper
and mix together thoroughly. Alternatively, put
the ingredients in a screw-top jar, replace the
lid and shake well.

Combine the lemon rind, vinegar, tarragon,
mustard and sugar in a small bowl and add
salt and pepper to taste. Stir to mix, then
gradually whisk in the oil. Alternatively, mix all
the ingredients in a screw-top jar and shake
well to combine.

tarragon & lemon dressing

Makes 50 ml (2 fl oz)
Preparation time 5 minutes

finely grated rind of 1 **lemon**
2 tablespoons **tarragon vinegar** (see below)
1 tablespoon chopped **tarragon**
¼ teaspoon **Dijon mustard**
pinch of **caster sugar**
5 tablespoons **olive oil**
salt and **pepper**

tarragon vinegar

Makes 500 ml (17 fl oz)
Preparation time 5 minutes

500 ml (17 fl oz) **white wine vinegar**
2 sprigs of **tarragon**

Put the vinegar into a clean glass bottle and
add the sprigs of tarragon. Seal and leave
for at least 2 days. The flavour will improve
with time.

basil-flavoured oil

Makes 400 ml (14 fl oz)
Preparation time 15 minutes

bunch of **basil**
400 ml (14 fl oz) **olive oil**

Blanch the basil in boiling water for
30 seconds, then refresh in cold water.
Squeeze out any excess water from the basil
and chop it roughly. Put the basil in a food
processor or blender with the oil and whiz
until smooth. Pour the oil through a fine sieve
into a clean, dry bottle, seal and leave
overnight, when the sediment will have settled
and you will be left with a bright green,
basil-flavoured oil.

mint & yogurt dressing

Makes 100 ml (3½ fl oz)
Preparation time 5 minutes

½ small **cucumber**, peeled
1 tablespoon **olive oil**
4 tablespoons **natural yogurt**
2 tablespoons chopped **mint**
salt and **pepper**

Cut the cucumber in half lengthways and
remove the seeds with a teaspoon. Finely
chop the flesh.

Mix the cucumber with the oil, yogurt and
chopped mint and season to taste with salt
(if liked) and pepper.

plum sauce

Serves 4
Preparation time 15 minutes
Cooking time 15–18 minutes

250 g (8 oz) **plums**
150 ml (¼ pint) **vegetable stock**
5 tablespoons **port** (optional)
1 teaspoon **allspice**
2 teaspoons **soy sauce**
1 tablespoon **cornflour**

Peel, stone and roughly chop the plums and
put them in a saucepan with the stock, port
(if used), allspice and soy sauce. Bring to the
boil and simmer for 10–15 minutes until the
plums are soft. Transfer to a food processor
or blender and whiz until smooth. Return the
plum mixture to the saucepan and stir in the
cornflour with about 2 tablespoons water to
make a thick sauce. Keep warm until needed.

side salads

chicory & baby cos salad

Serves **4**
Preparation time **10 minutes**

2 **chicory heads**, white and
    red if possible, about 175 g
    (6 oz) in total
3 **baby cos lettuce hearts**

Dressing
50 g (2 oz) **Gorgonzola
    cheese**
1 tablespoon **Worcestershire
    sauce**
2 tablespoons **Mayonnaise**
    (see page 12)
2 tablespoons **soured cream**
3 tablespoons **olive oil**
1 tablespoon **white wine
    vinegar**
2 tablespoons **lemon juice**
salt and **pepper**

Slice the base of the chicory heads and the lettuces and carefully remove the individual leaves. Put the leaves in a large salad bowl.

Make the dressing by whisking together all the ingredients. Season to taste with salt and pepper.

Add the dressing to the lettuce and chicory leaves, toss briefly to mix and serve.

For Gorgonzola, pecan & pear salad, prepare the salad leaves in the same way as above. Add 50 g (2 oz) toasted pecan nuts and 1 finely sliced pear to the chicory and lettuce leaves. Toss well. Whisk the dressing ingredients as above, toss through the salad and serve immediately.

coleslaw

Serves **4**

Preparation time **15 minutes, plus standing**

½ **white cabbage**
¼ **red cabbage**
2 **carrots**
1 **red onion**
2 tablespoons roughly chopped **parsley**

Dressing
300 ml (½ pint) **Mayonnaise** (see page 12)
1 tablespoon **white wine vinegar**
½ teaspoon **caster sugar**
salt and **pepper**

Finely shred both cabbages and the carrots and finely slice the onion. Mix the cabbages and carrots in a large salad bowl with the onion and parsley.

Make the dressing by whisking the mayonnaise, vinegar and sugar and season to taste with salt and pepper. Toss the dressing through the cabbage mixture, then leave to stand for at least 30 minutes before serving.

For apple & radish slaw, add 1 finely sliced red apple and 5 finely sliced radishes to the coleslaw ingredients. Instead of the mayonnaise dressing, whisk together 1 teaspoon Dijon mustard, 2 tablespoons white wine vinegar and 3 tablespoons olive oil. Add the dressing to the salad, cover and leave in the refrigerator for at least 30 minutes before serving.

rocket, pear & pecorino salad

Serves **4**
Preparation time **10 minutes**

250 g (8 oz) **rocket**
2 **pears**
75 g (3 oz) **pepper pecorino cheese**, cut into shavings

Dressing
1 teaspoon **Dijon mustard**
2 tablespoons **cider vinegar**
2 tablespoons **olive oil**
salt and **pepper**

Make the dressing by whisking the mustard, cider vinegar and oil. Season to taste with salt and pepper.

Put the rocket in a large salad bowl. Finely slice the pear and add it to the rocket. Add the dressing to the salad and toss carefully to mix.

Layer most of the shavings of the pecorino through the rocket and pear salad, garnish with the remaining shavings and serve.

For rocket, apple & balsamic salad, combine 250 g (8 oz) rocket, 1 finely sliced green apple and 75 g (3 oz) shaved pecorino cheese in a large salad bowl. Whisk together 2 tablespoons aged balsamic vinegar and 3 tablespoons olive oil. Add the dressing to the salad, toss carefully to mix and serve immediately.

green salad

Serves **4–6**
Preparation time **5 minutes**

400 g (13 oz) **mixed baby
leaves and herbs**, such as
**watercress, frisée (curly-
leaved endive), rocket,
tatsoi** or **spinach, chives,
parsley** and **chervil**

Dressing
1 teaspoon **Dijon mustard**
2 tablespoons **chardonnay
vinegar**
4 tablespoons **olive oil**
salt and **pepper**

Make the dressing by whisking together the mustard,
vinegar and oil. Season to taste with salt and pepper.

Put the mixed leaves into a large salad bowl. Carefully
toss the leaves and herbs with the dressing to combine
and serve immediately.

For green salad with crusted goats' cheese, mix
together 75 g (3 oz) breadcrumbs, 20 g (¾ oz)
crushed hazelnuts, 2 tablespoons chopped parsley
and 1 crushed garlic clove. Season to taste with salt
and pepper. Cut 100 g (3½ oz) goats' cheese into
rounds, dip them in flour, then in lightly beaten egg,
then in the breadcrumb mixture. Heat 2 tablespoons
vegetable oil in a large frying pan over a medium heat
and fry the cheese slices for 3 minutes on each side
until golden and crispy. Drain on kitchen paper and
serve with the green salad as above.

garden salad

Serves **4**
Preparation time **10 minutes**

½ **cucumber**
250 g (8 oz) **cherry tomatoes**
250 g (8 oz) **baby leaf mix**,
   such as **mizuna, baby
   chard, lollo rosso, purslane**
   and **oak-leaf lettuce**
1 **avocado**
50 g (2 oz) pitted **black olives**

Dressing
1 teaspoon **Dijon mustard**
2 tablespoons **cider vinegar**
3 tablespoons **olive oil**
salt and **pepper**

Peel and slice the cucumber and halve the tomatoes. Mix the salad leaves with the cucumber and tomatoes in a large salad bowl. Stone and peel the avocado, cut the flesh into dice and add to the bowl with the olives.

Make the dressing by whisking together the mustard, vinegar and oil. Season to taste with salt and pepper.

Pour the dressing over the salad, toss carefully to combine and serve.

For garden salad with grilled chicken, mix together the grated rind of 1 lemon, 1 tablespoon chopped parsley, 1 crushed garlic clove, 2 tablespoons olive oil and salt and pepper. Coat 2 chicken breasts, each about 125 g (4 oz), in the mixture and place on a foil-lined baking sheet. Cook under a preheated hot grill for 3–4 minutes on each side until cooked through. Slice the chicken breasts and arrange neatly on top of the garden salad.

courgette, feta & mint salad

Serves **4–6**
Preparation time **10 minutes**
Cooking time **10 minutes**

3 **green courgettes**
2 **yellow courgettes**
olive oil
small bunch of **mint**
40 g (1½ oz) **feta cheese**
salt and **pepper**

Dressing
2 tablespoons **olive oil**
grated **rind** and **juice** of
   1 **lemon**

Slice the courgettes thinly lengthways into long ribbons. Drizzle with oil and season with salt and pepper. Heat a griddle pan to very hot and grill the courgettes in batches until marked by the griddle on both sides, then place in a large salad bowl.

Make the dressing by whisking together the oil and the grated lemon rind and juice. Season to taste with salt the pepper.

Roughly chop the mint, reserving some leaves for garnish. Carefully mix together the courgettes, mint and dressing. Transfer them to a large salad bowl, then crumble the feta over the top, garnish with the remaining mint leaves and serve.

For marinated courgette salad, thinly slice 3 courgettes lengthways and put them in a non-metallic bowl with ½ deseeded and sliced red chilli, 4 tablespoons lemon juice, 1 crushed garlic clove and 4 tablespoons olive oil. Season to taste with salt and pepper. Leave the salad to marinate, covered, for at least 1 hour. Roughly chop a small bunch of mint, toss with the salad and serve immediately.

shaved fennel & radish salad

Serves **4—6**
Preparation time **10 minutes**

2 **fennel bulbs**, about
   650 g (1 lb 5 oz) in total
300 g (10 oz) **radishes**
2 tablespoons roughly
   chopped **parsley**

Dressing
4 tablespoons **lemon juice**
2 tablespoons **olive oil**
salt and **pepper**

Slice the fennel and radishes as thinly as possible on a mandolin or with a knife, reserving the fennel fronds for garnish. Toss together in a large salad bowl with the parsley.

Make the dressing by whisking together the lemon juice and oil. Season to taste with salt and pepper.

Add the dressing to the salad and toss gently to mix. Garnish with the feathery fennel tips and serve.

For pickled fennel salad, mix together 3 tablespoons cider vinegar, 1 tablespoon toasted cumin seeds and 400 ml (14 fl oz) water in a small saucepan. Bring to the boil and season to taste with salt and pepper. Immediately pour the liquid over 650 g (1 lb 5 oz) thinly sliced fennel and leave to cool. Drain the pickled fennel and serve as a side salad or as an accompaniment to grilled fish.

green beans with almonds

Serves **4**

Preparation time
  10 minutes, plus standing

Cooking time **5 minutes**

1 teaspoon **Dijon mustard**
2 tablespoons **white wine vinegar**
1 **shallot**, finely chopped
3 tablespoons **olive oil**
500 g (1 lb) **green beans**
2 tablespoons **toasted slivered almonds**

Mix together the mustard and vinegar in a bowl. Add the finely chopped shallot, and leave to stand for 10 minutes, then whisk in the oil.

Trim and blanch the beans, then toss them in the dressing and serve in a salad bowl topped with the slivered almonds.

For green beans with anchovy dressing, put 150 ml (¼ pint) olive oil into a small, heavy-based saucepan and add 3 canned anchovies. Cook over a low heat for 5 minutes until the anchovies have softened and broken down. Remove the pan from the heat and leave the dressing to cool to room temperature. Whisk in 2 tablespoons white wine vinegar and some cracked black pepper. Toss 500 g (1 lb) trimmed and blanched green beans in the dressing and serve immediately.

pickled vegetable salad

Serves **4**
Preparation time **20 minutes,
plus cooling**
Cooking time **20 minutes**

8 small **shallots**
1 small **cauliflower**
1 **red pepper**
1 litre (1¾ pints) **water**
150 ml (¼ pint) **white wine
vinegar**
150 g (5 oz) **green beans**
150 g (5 oz) **sugar snap
peas**
75 g (3 oz) **watercress**
olive oil
salt and **pepper**

Trim the shallots and break the cauliflower into small
florets. Core and deseed the pepper and cut the flesh
into 2 cm (¾ inch) squares.

Put the water and vinegar into a heavy-based
saucepan, bring to the boil and add the cauliflower,
pepper and shallots. Return the liquid to the boil and
boil for 2 minutes. Take the saucepan off the heat
and leave the vegetables to cool in the liquid.

Trim the beans and sugar snap peas and blanch in
lightly salted boiling water. Refresh them in cold water
and drain.

When the pickling liquid is cool, strain the vegetables
and mix them with the beans, peas and watercress in
a large salad bowl. Dress with olive oil, season to taste
with salt and pepper and serve.

For pickled cucumber & chilli salad, cut
2 cucumbers in half lengthways and remove the
seeds by running a small teaspoon along the centre.
Slice the cucumber diagonally and place in a non-
metallic bowl. Add 1 tablespoon finely sliced pickled
ginger, 1 deseeded and finely sliced red chilli and
5 finely sliced spring onions. Put 100 g (3½ oz) sugar,
75 ml (3 fl oz) rice wine vinegar and 400 ml (14 fl oz)
water in a heavy-based saucepan and bring to the
boil. Allow to cool, then pour the liquid over the
cucumbers and leave to stand for at least 1 hour.
The pickled cucumbers will keep for up to one week
in a covered container in the refrigerator.

potato salad

Serves **4–6**

Preparation time **10 minutes, plus cooling**

Cooking time **15 minutes**

1 kg (2 lb) **new potatoes**
125 g (4 oz) **smoked streaky bacon**
1 teaspoon **vegetable oil**
6 **spring onions**
175 ml (6 fl oz) **Mayonnaise** (see page 12)
salt and **pepper**

Halve the potatoes and cook in lightly salted boiling water until tender. Rinse under cold water and leave to cool.

Meanwhile, slice the bacon into thin strips. Heat the oil in a frying pan and cook the bacon until golden; drain on kitchen paper and allow to cool. Finely slice the spring onions, reserving some for garnish.

Put the potatoes, finely sliced spring onions and bacon in a large salad bowl. Gently stir in the mayonnaise. Season to taste with salt and pepper, garnish with the reserved spring onions and serve.

For blue cheese & walnut potato salad, add 50 g (2 oz) blue cheese, 2 tablespoon soured cream and 1 tablespoon lemon juice to 175 ml (6 fl oz) mayonnaise and combine well. Mix the dressing through the cooked potatoes together with 2 tablespoons chopped parsley. Garnish with 40 g (1½ oz) toasted walnuts and serve.

red cabbage slaw

Serves **4–6**

Preparation time **20 minutes**, plus marinating

500 g (1 lb) **red cabbage**
1 **red onion**
1 **raw beetroot**
2 **carrots**
1 **fennel bulb**
2 tablespoons chopped **parsley** or **dill**
75 g (3 oz) **raisins** or **sultanas**

Dressing

6 tablespoons **natural yogurt**
1 tablespoon **cider vinegar** or **white wine vinegar**
2 teaspoons **sweet German mustard** or **Dijon mustard**
1 teaspoon **clear honey**
1 **garlic clove**, crushed
salt and **pepper**

Trim the stalk end of the red cabbage and finely shred the cabbage. Cut the red onion in half and slice it thinly. Peel the beetroot and carrots and cut them both into thin matchsticks or grate coarsely. Halve the fennel bulb and shred it finely.

Put all the prepared vegetables, chopped parsley or dill and raisins or sultanas in a large salad bowl and toss them with your hands to combine well.

Make the dressing. Mix the yogurt with the vinegar, mustard, honey, crushed garlic, a pinch of salt and plenty of pepper. Pour this dressing over the slaw, mix well and leave to marinate for at least 1 hour. Serve the slaw with rye or sourdough bread.

For crunchy chilli slaw, finely slice 250 g (8 oz) white cabbage and 250 g (8 oz) red cabbage. Cut 1 carrot into thin ribbons with a peeler and thinly slice 1 red onion and 1 fennel bulb. Make a dressing by mixing together 3 tablespoons sweet chilli sauce, 1 tablespoon soy sauce, 1 tablespoon barbecue sauce, 2 tablespoons olive oil and the juice of 2 limes. Toss the salad in the dressing and allow to stand for at least 30 minutes for the flavours to infuse before serving.

rocket & parmesan salad

Serves **4–6**, as a side dish
Preparation time **5 minutes**

250 g (8 oz) **rocket**
20 g (¾ oz) **finely grated
  Parmesan cheese**
40 g (1½ oz) **Parmesan
  cheese shavings**

Dressing
4 tablespoons **lemon juice**
2 tablespoons **olive oil**
½ teaspoon **Dijon mustard**
salt and **pepper**

Make the dressing by whisking the lemon juice, oil and mustard. Season to taste with salt and pepper.

Put the rocket in a large salad bowl, sprinkle over the Parmesan and mix lightly. Pour over the dressing and toss to combine. Garnish the salad with the Parmesan shavings and serve.

For rocket salad with chive dressing, blanch a bunch of chives in boiling water for 30 seconds until bright green. Refresh immediately in cold water. Squeeze out all the excess water, roughly chop and transfer to a blender jug. Add 50 ml (2 fl oz) Mayonnaise (see page 12), 1 tablespoon white wine vinegar and salt and pepper to taste. Blend until smooth, adjusting the consistency with 1 tablespoon warm water if necessary. Mix 250 g (8 oz) rocket with a thinly sliced fennel bulb, pour over the dressing, toss together and serve immediately.

light salads

caesar salad

Serves **4–6**
Preparation time **20 minutes**
Cooking time **12 minutes**

1 **cos lettuce**
50 g (2 oz) can **anchovy
    fillets in olive oil**
1 small **white loaf**
75 g (3 oz) **butter**
3 tablespoons **Parmesan
    cheese shavings**, to garnish

Dressing
5 tablespoons **Mayonnaise**
    (see page 12)
4–5 tablespoons **water**
1–2 **garlic cloves**
3 tablespoons finely grated
    Parmesan cheese
salt and **pepper**

Make the dressing. Put the mayonnaise in a small bowl and stir in enough of the water to make a thin, pourable sauce. Pound the garlic to a paste with a little coarse sea salt. Add to the mayonnaise with the Parmesan and stir well. Thin with a little more water if necessary so that the sauce remains pourable. Add pepper to taste and set aside.

Tear the lettuce leaves into bite-sized pieces and put them into a large salad bowl. Drain the anchovies, chop them into small pieces and scatter over the lettuce.

Cut the bread into 3 cm (1¼ inch) thick slices. Discard the crusts. Melt the butter, brush the slices of bread then cut the bread into 2.5 cm (1 inch) squares. Brush a baking sheet with a little melted butter and arrange the bread in a single layer, brushing the sides with any remaining butter. Bake in a preheated oven, 200°C (400°F), Gas Mark 6, for about 12 minutes or until the croûtons are crisp and a deep golden colour. Watch the croûtons carefully after 8 minutes, because they tend to colour quickly towards the end of the cooking time.

Tip the hot croûtons into the salad and quickly drizzle the dressing over the top. Scatter the Parmesan shavings over the salad and serve immediately.

For cajun chicken Caesar salad, mix 2 teaspoons cajun seasoning with 4 tablespoons olive oil. Rub 4 chicken breasts in the mixture and allow to marinate for 1 hour in the refrigerator. Heat a griddle pan over a medium heat and cook the chicken for 4–5 minutes on each side until cooked through. Allow to rest for 2 minutes, then slice thinly and serve with Caesar Salad.

greek salad

Serves **2**

Preparation time **10–15 minutes**

½ **cucumber**

4 **plum tomatoes**

1 **red pepper**

1 **green pepper**

½ **red onion**

60 g (2¼ oz) **pitted Kalamata olives**

50 g (2 oz) **feta cheese**, diced

Dressing

4 tablespoons **olive oil**

1 tablespoon chopped **parsley**

salt and **pepper**

Cut the cucumber and tomatoes into 1–2 cm (½–¾ inch) chunks and put them in a large salad bowl. Cut the flesh from the peppers and carefully remove the ribs and the seeds. Cut the pepper flesh into thin strips and put them in the bowl with the cucumbers and tomatoes. Finely slice the red onion and add to the bowl with the olives.

Make the dressing by whisking the oil and parsley. Season to taste with salt and pepper.

Pour the dressing over the salad and toss carefully. Transfer to serving bowls, scatter some feta evenly over each bowl and serve.

For Greek salad with garlic pitta bread, rub 4 pitta breads with a peeled clove of garlic, drizzle with olive oil, season with salt and pepper and toast in a preheated oven, 190°C (375°F), Gas Mark 5, for 4–5 minutes until crisp. Roughly break the pitta breads into pieces, about 2 cm (¾ inch) square, and set aside. Prepare the Greek Salad as above, adding 2 tablespoons chopped basil and 2 tablespoons chopped mint. Toss the salad and serve, garnished with the pitta bread pieces and a dollop of hummus on each plate.

niçoise salad

Serves **4**
Preparation time **15 minutes**
Cooking time **10–15 minutes**

400 g (13 oz) small **potatoes**
200 g (7 oz) **green beans**,
   trimmed
5 large **plum tomatoes**
2 tablespoons chopped
   parsley, plus extra leaves
   for garnish
60 g (2¼ oz) **pitted black
   olives**
2 tablespoons **lemon juice**
2–3 tablespoons **olive oil**
4 large, **soft-poached eggs**
salt and **pepper**

Cook the potatoes in lightly salted boiling water, leave them to cool and halve them. Meanwhile, bring a large saucepan of lightly salted water to the boil, add the trimmed green beans and blanch for 1–2 minutes until bright green and still firm to the touch. Refresh in cold water, drain and transfer to a large salad bowl.

Core the tomatoes and cut each one into 6 pieces. Add the tomatoes and chopped parsley to the beans with the potatoes, olives, lemon juice and oil. Season to taste with salt and pepper.

Transfer the salad to serving plates and top each one with a poached egg cut in half and a drizzle of olive oil. Garnish with the reserved parsley leaves and serve.

For tuna niçoise salad, prepare the salad in the same way as the niçoise salad. Drain 185 g (6¼ oz) canned tuna in olive oil. Flake the fish and toss it through the niçoise salad and serve, topped with a soft-poached egg, if liked.

turkey & avocado salad

Serves **4**
Preparation time **20 minutes**

375 g (12 oz) cooked **turkey**
1 large **avocado**
punnet of **mustard** and **cress**
150 g (5 oz) **mixed salad
  leaves**
50 g (2 oz) **mixed toasted
  seeds,** such as **pumpkin**
  and **sunflower**

Dressing
2 tablespoons **apple juice**
2 tablespoons **natural yogurt**
1 teaspoon **clear honey**
1 teaspoon **wholegrain
  mustard**
salt and **pepper**

Thinly slice the turkey. Peel, stone and dice the
avocado and mix it with the mustard and cress and
salad leaves in a large bowl. Add the turkey and
toasted seeds and stir to combine.

Make the dressing by whisking together the apple
juice, yogurt, honey and mustard. Season to taste with
salt and pepper. .

Pour the dressing over the salad and toss to coat.
Serve the salad with toasted wholegrain rye bread or
rolled up in flat breads.

For crab, apple & avocado salad, prepare the salad
in the same way, using 300 g (10 oz) cooked, fresh
white crab meat instead of the turkey. Cut 1 apple into
thin matchsticks and toss with a little lemon juice to
stop it from discolouring. Make a dressing by whisking
2 tablespoons apple juice with 3 tablespoons olive oil,
a squeeze of lemon juice and 1 finely diced shallot.
Season to taste with salt and pepper. Pour the
dressing over the salad, stir carefully to mix and serve.

panzanella salad

Serves **4**

Preparation time **15 minutes**, plus standing

600 g (1¼ lb) large **tomatoes**
1 tablespoon **sea salt**
150 g (5 oz) **ciabatta bread**
½ **red onion**, finely chopped
1 handful of **basil leaves**, plus extra for garnish
1 tablespoon **red wine vinegar**
2 tablespoons **olive oil**
12 **pickled white anchovies**, drained
salt and **pepper**

Roughly chop the tomatoes into 2 cm (¾ inch) pieces and put them in a non-metallic bowl. Sprinkle over the sea salt and leave to stand for 1 hour.

Remove the crusts from the ciabatta and tear the bread into rough chunks.

Give the tomatoes a good squash with clean hands, then add the bread, onion, basil, vinegar and oil. Season to taste with salt and pepper. Mix together carefully and transfer to serving plates. Garnish with the drained anchovies and the reserved basil and serve.

For tomato & bean salad, finely slice 1 red onion, cover with 4 tablespoons red wine vinegar and leave to stand for about 30 minutes. Cut 150 g (5 oz) ciabatta bread into chunks and place in a roasting tin. Drizzle with olive oil, season with salt and pepper and add 2 sprigs of thyme. Cook the ciabatta in a preheated oven, 190°C (375°F), Gas Mark 5, until golden and crispy. Dice 300 g (10 oz) tomatoes and put them in a large bowl. Add 410 g (13½ oz) can borlotti beans, rinsed and drained, 410 g (13½ oz) can cannellini beans, rinsed and drained, and 1 bunch of chopped basil. Remove the onion from the vinegar, reserving the vinegar, and add to the salad with 12 drained pickled white anchovies. Add 1 teaspoon Dijon mustard to the reserved vinegar and whisk in 5 tablespoons olive oil. Season with salt and pepper. Add the dressing to the salad, toss thoroughly and serve, garnished with the ciabatta croûtons.

spring vegetable salad

Serves **4**
Preparation time **10 minutes**
Cooking time **10 minutes**

200 g (7 oz) fresh or frozen
  peas
200 g (7 oz) **asparagus**,
  trimmed
200 g (7 oz) **sugar snap
  peas**
2 **courgettes**
1 **fennel bulb**

Dressing
grated **rind** and **juice** of
  1 **lemon**
1 teaspoon **Dijon mustard**
1 teaspoon **clear honey**
1 tablespoon chopped **flat
  leaf parsley**
1 tablespoon **olive oil**

Put the peas, asparagus and sugar snap peas in a saucepan of salted boiling water and simmer for 3 minutes. Drain, then refresh under cold running water.

Cut the courgettes into long, thin ribbons and thinly slice the fennel. Transfer all the vegetables to a large salad bowl and mix together.

Make the dressing by whisking together the lemon rind and juice, mustard, honey, parsley and oil in another bowl. Toss the dressing through the vegetables and serve.

For beetroot dressing, to serve with spring vegetable salad, prepare the vegetables as above and set aside. Finely slice ½ red onion and 1 garlic clove. Heat 2 tablespoons olive oil in a saucepan over a medium heat and gently cook the onion and garlic. Add 4 precooked beetroot and 6 roughly chopped sun-blushed tomatoes and continue to cook for 3 minutes. When the onions start to colour deglaze the pan with 2 tablespoons balsamic vinegar. Cook for 1 minute, then add 100 ml (3½ fl oz) chicken or vegetable stock. Reduce the stock by a quarter, then leave to cool. Transfer the stock to a food processor or blender and whiz until smooth. Season with salt and pepper and add up to 2 tablespoons cream until the dressing reaches a drizzling consistency. Drizzle the dressing over the vegetables and serve.

beetroot & orange salad

Serves **2–4**
Preparation time **15 minutes**
Cooking time **30 minutes**

7 small **beetroot**
1 teaspoon **cumin seeds**
1 tablespoon **red wine vinegar**
2 **oranges**
65 g (2½ oz) **watercress**
75 g (3 oz) **soft goats' cheese**
cracked black pepper

Dressing
1 tablespoon **clear honey**
1 teaspoon **wholegrain mustard**
1½ tablespoons **white wine vinegar**
3 tablespoons **olive oil**
salt and **pepper**

Scrub and trim the beetroot and put them in a foil-lined roasting tin with the cumin seeds and vinegar and bake in a preheated oven, 190°C (375°F), Gas Mark 5, for 30 minutes or until cooked. Check by piercing one with a knife. Allow the beetroot to cool slightly and then, wearing food-handling gloves, rub off the skin and slice the globes into halves, or quarters if large.

Meanwhile, peel and segment the oranges. Make the dressing by whisking the honey, mustard, vinegar and oil. Season to taste with salt and pepper.

Put the watercress in a bowl with the beetroot and add the dressing. Mix gently to combine. Arrange the oranges on a plate, top with the salad and crumble over the cheese. Season with cracked black pepper and serve.

For marinated goats' cheese, sun-blushed tomato & salami salad, in a small plastic container cover 125 g (4 oz) soft goats' cheese with about 250 ml (8 fl oz) olive oil. Add 2 sliced garlic cloves, 1 piece lemon rind, a sprig of thyme and 1 tablespoon toasted cumin seeds. Leave to marinate overnight. Drain the cheese, discarding the marinade, and leave to dry on kitchen paper. Thinly slice 125 g (4 oz) salami and place in a large salad bowl with 150 g (5 oz) drained sun-blushed tomatoes and 150 g (5 oz) rocket. Crumble 60 g (2¼ oz) of the goats' cheese into the salad. Make the dressing as above and pour over the salad. Toss carefully to combine, crumble the remaining goats' cheese over the top and serve.

cajun potato & prawn salad

Serves **2**
Preparation time **10 minutes**
Cooking time **15–20 minutes**

300 g (10 oz) **new potatoes**
1 tablespoon **olive oil**
250 g (8 oz) **cooked peeled king prawns**
1 **garlic clove**, crushed
4 **spring onions**, finely sliced
2 teaspoons **cajun seasoning**
1 ripe **avocado**
handful of **alfalfa sprouts**
salt

Halve the potatoes and cook them in a large saucepan of lightly salted boiling water for 10–15 minutes or until tender. Drain well.

Heat the oil in a wok or large, nonstick frying pan. Add the prawns, crushed garlic, finely sliced spring onions and cajun seasoning and stir-fry for 2–3 minutes or until the prawns are hot. Stir in the potatoes and cook for 1 minute. Transfer to a serving dish.

Peel, stone and dice the avocado and stir into the salad. Top with the alfalfa sprouts and serve.

For cajun chicken wings with potato & avocado salad, mix together 2 tablespoons vegetable oil and 2 teaspoons cajun seasoning. Marinate 12 chicken wings in the mixture for at least 1 hour. Put the chicken wings on a foil-lined baking sheet and cook under a preheated hot grill for 8–10 minutes until golden and cooked through. Prepare the potatoes as above and stir-fry in a wok or nonstick frying pan with 1 crushed garlic clove, 4 sliced spring onions and 2 teaspoons cajun spice. Mix with the avocado and serve with a wedge of lettuce and the chicken wings.

pea & broad bean salad

Serves **4**
Preparation time **15 minutes**
Cooking time **10 minutes**

150 g (5 oz) frozen **peas**
150 g (5 oz) **broad beans**
75 g (3 oz) **snow pea tendrils**
small bunch of **mint**, roughly
   chopped
150 g (5 oz) **feta cheese**

Dressing
1 teaspoon **Dijon mustard**
2 tablespoons **olive oil**
1 tablespoon **chardonnay
   vinegar**
salt and **pepper**

Bring a large saucepan of lightly salted water to the boil and cook the peas for 2 minutes. Refresh in cold water. Cook the broad beans for 3 minutes, refresh and peel to reveal the bright green inside. Mix the peas and broad beans with the snow pea tendrils and roughly chopped mint.

Make the dressing by whisking the mustard, oil and vinegar. Season to taste with salt and pepper.

Crumble the feta into the salad, carefully mix in the dressing and serve.

For pea, broad bean & chorizo salad, prepare the peas and broad beans in the same way as above. Put them in a bowl with the snow pea tendrils and add 1 grated courgette. Thinly slice 3 chorizo sausages diagonally and fry in a hot frying pan until golden and crispy. Drain on kitchen paper, then add to the salad. Whisk the dressing ingredients as above and toss the salad with the mint and feta. Serve immediately.

orange & avocado salad

Serves **4**

Preparation time **20 minutes**

4 large juicy **oranges**
2 small ripe **avocados**
2 teaspoons **cardamom pods**
3 tablespoons **olive oil**
1 tablespoon **clear honey**
pinch of **allspice**
2 teaspoons **lemon juice**
salt and **pepper**
sprigs of **watercress**, to
   garnish

Cut the skin and the white membrane off the oranges. Working over a bowl to catch the juice, cut between the membranes to remove the segments. Peel and stone the avocados, slice the flesh and toss gently with the orange segments. Pile on to serving plates.

Reserve a few whole cardamom pods for garnishing. Crush the remainder using a mortar and pestle to extract the seeds or place them in a small bowl and crush with the end of a rolling pin. Pick out and discard the pods.

Mix the seeds with the oil, honey, allspice and lemon juice. Season to taste with salt and pepper and stir in the reserved orange juice. Garnish the salads with sprigs of watercress and the reserved cardamom pods and serve with the dressing spooned over the top.

For orange, avocado & honey duck salad, prepare the salad as above. Score 4 duck breasts with a diamond pattern on the fat side of the breast. Place the duck, skin side down, in a large frying pan, season with salt and pepper and cook for 5–6 minutes until golden. Turn the duck over, drizzle with honey and cook for a further 6 minutes or until cooked through. Set aside and allow to rest for 10 minutes. Slice the duck and serve with the orange and avocado salad.

smoked trout & grape salad

Serves **2**
Preparation time **15 minutes**

200 g (7 oz) **smoked trout**
160 g (5½ oz) **red seedless grapes**
75 g (3 oz) **watercress**
1 **fennel bulb**

Dressing
3 tablespoons **Mayonnaise** (see page 12)
4 **cornichons**, finely diced
1½ tablespoons **capers**, chopped
2 tablespoons **lemon juice**
salt and **pepper**

Flake the smoked trout into bite-sized pieces, removing any bones, and place in a large salad bowl.

Wash and drain the grapes and watercress and add them to the bowl. Finely slice the fennel and add to the mix.

Make the dressing by mixing the mayonnaise, cornichons, capers and lemon juice. Season to taste with salt and pepper, then carefully mix through the salad and serve.

For crispy trout salad, add 1 finely chopped hard-boiled egg, 2 finely chopped anchovy fillets and 1 tablespoon chopped parsley to the dressing. Prepare the salad as above, adding 1 green apple, cut into matchsticks. Season 2 pieces of fresh trout, each about 140 g (4½ oz), with salt and pepper. Heat 1 tablespoon vegetable oil in a frying pan over a high heat and cook the trout, skin side down, for 4 minutes, pressing it down with a fish slice to give an evenly crispy skin. Turn over the fish and cook for a further 2 minutes or until it is just cooked through. Remove from the pan. Toss the salad with the dressing and serve immediately with the crispy trout.

watermelon & feta salad

Serves **4**

Preparation time **10 minutes**

Cooking time **2 minutes**

1 tablespoon **black sesame seeds**

500 g (1 lb) **watermelon**

175 g (6 oz) **feta cheese**

875 g (1¾ lb) **rocket**

sprigs of **mint**, **parsley** and **coriander**

6 tablespoons **olive oil**

1 tablespoon **orange flower water**

1½ tablespoons **lemon juice**

1 teaspoon **pomegranate syrup** (optional)

½ teaspoon **caster sugar**

salt and **pepper**

Heat a frying pan and dry-fry the sesame seeds for 2 minutes until aromatic, then set aside.

Peel, deseed and dice the watermelon and dice the feta. Arrange the watermelon and feta on a large plate with the rocket and herbs.

Whisk together the oil, orange flower water, lemon juice, pomegranate syrup (if used) and sugar. Season to taste with salt and pepper, then drizzle over the salad. Sprinkle with the sesame seeds and serve.

For tomato, feta & basil salad, cut 750 g (1½ lb) tomatoes into wedges and carefully transfer them to a large salad bowl. Make the dressing by whisking together in a small bowl 3 tablespoons aged balsamic vinegar and 6 tablespoons olive oil. Add 875 g (1¾ lb) rocket, a small handful of basil leaves and the sprigs of mint and parsley to the tomatoes. Crumble over 175 g (6 oz) feta cheese, drizzle over the dressing and combine lightly. Garnish with 3 tablespoons toasted pine nuts and serve.

chicken, apricot & almond salad

Serves **4**

Preparation time **10 minutes**

200 g (7 oz) **celery**

75 g (3 oz) **almonds**

3 tablespoons chopped
parsley

4 tablespoons **Mayonnaise**
(see page 12)

3 poached or roasted **chicken
breasts**, each about 150 g
(5 oz)

12 fresh **apricots**

salt and **pepper**

Thinly slice the celery sticks diagonally, reserving the yellow inner leaves. Transfer to a large salad bowl together with half the leaves. Roughly chop the almonds and add half to the bowl with the parsley and mayonnaise. Season to taste with salt and pepper.

Arrange the salad on a serving plate. Shred the chicken and halve and stone the apricots. Add the chicken and apricots to the salad and stir lightly to combine. Garnish with the remaining almonds and celery leaves and serve.

For grilled chicken with apricot & tomato salad,

marinate 4 chicken breasts, each about 150 g (5 oz), with 2 crushed garlic cloves, 50 ml (2 fl oz) sweet chilli sauce and the juice and rind of 1 lime for at least 1 hour. Remove the chicken from the marinade and transfer to a heated griddle pan. Cook until golden and cooked through. Remove the stones and chop 12 apricots into 5 mm (¼ inch) pieces. Mix with 3 ripe tomatoes cut into 5 mm (¼ inch) pieces and 2 tablespoons chopped coriander. Whisk together 3 tablespoons red wine vinegar, 3 tablespoons olive oil, 1 teaspoon brown sugar and 1 teaspoon soy sauce and pour the dressing over the salad. Combine well and serve with the chicken.

daikon, carrot & red pepper salad

Serves **4**
Preparation time **15 minutes**
Cooking time **2–3 minutes**

1 small **daikon**
3 **carrots**
1 large, firm **red pepper**
1 tablespoon **toasted
  sesame seeds**
1 teaspoon **sesame oil**
1 tablespoon **mirin**
1 tablespoon **rice wine
  vinegar**
4 **spring onions**, finely
  shredded
coriander leaves, to garnish

Grate or shred the daikon, carrots and red pepper. If
the red pepper proves difficult to shred, thinly slice it into
julienne strips. Place the vegetables and the sesame
seeds in a bowl and mix together with your hands.

Put the sesame oil, mirin and vinegar in a small pan
and heat gently for 2–3 minutes to blend the flavours.
Remove the pan from the heat and allow the mixture to
cool a little.

Arrange the salad in a mound in the centre of each of
4 plates and pour the dressing over and around it. Top
each salad with finely shredded spring onions, garnish
with coriander leaves and serve.

For daikon salad with Asian-style ribs, make
a marinade in a small saucepan by combining
5 tablespoons soy sauce, 2 tablespoons brown sugar,
2 tablespoons rice wine vinegar, 1 cm (½ inch) fresh
root ginger, peeled and sliced, the rind and juice of
1 orange, 1 cinnamon stick and 1 star anise. Warm
the marinade thoroughly, stirring until the sugar has
dissolved, then allow to cool. Cut 600 g (1 lb 2 oz)
pork spare ribs into pieces, pour the marinade over
them and leave to marinate overnight. Arrange the
spare ribs on a foil-lined baking sheet and grill for
20 minutes until sticky, rotating and basting
occasionally. Prepare the salad as above and serve
with the cooked ribs.

fattoush

Serves **4—6**
Preparation time **15 minutes**
Cooking time **5 minutes**

5 ripe **tomatoes**
1 **cucumber**
1 **green pepper**
1 **red pepper**
½ **red onion**
4 **flat breads**
2 tablespoons **olive oil**
salt and **pepper**

Dressing
1 **garlic clove**, crushed
4 tablespoons **lemon juice**
3 tablespoons **olive oil**
2 tablespoons chopped
   parsley
2 tablespoons chopped **mint**

Cut the tomatoes, cucumber, green and red peppers and onion into 1 cm (½ inch) pieces and put them in a non-metallic bowl.

Cut the flat breads into 1 cm (½ inch) squares. Heat the oil in a frying pan and fry the bread in batches. Drain on kitchen paper and allow to cool.

Make the dressing by whisking together the garlic, lemon juice, oil, parsley and mint.

Pour the dressing over the vegetables, toss carefully and season to taste with salt and pepper. Garnish with the croûtons and serve immediately.

For whole grilled sardines with fattoush salad, gut and bone 8 whole sardines and put them on a baking sheet. Put 1 sprig of rosemary in each cavity. Mix together 4 tablespoons olive oil and 1 crushed garlic clove and brush the sardines with the garlic-flavoured oil. Season to taste with salt and pepper. Cook the sardines on a barbecue or under a preheated hot grill for 3 minutes on each side. Remove the sardines from the grill and serve with the fattoush salad and wedges of lemon.

fig, raspberry & prosciutto salad

Serves **4—6**
Preparation time **5 minutes**

150 g (5 oz) **rocket and
  beetroot salad mix**
6 ripe **figs**, halved
150 g (5 oz) **raspberries**
8 slices of **prosciutto**
2 large **buffalo mozzarella
  balls**, each about
  150 g (5 oz)

Dressing
2 tablespoons **aged balsamic
  vinegar**
2 tablespoons **olive oil**

Put the rocket and beetroot leaves in a large bowl, add
the halved figs, the raspberries and the prosciutto, toss
carefully and transfer to a large serving plate.

Make the dressing by whisking together the vinegar
and oil. Tear each mozzarella ball into 3 pieces and
arrange them on the salad. Drizzle the dressing over
the salad and serve.

For grilled fig & raspberry fruit salad, cut 6 ripe
figs in half and sprinkle ½ tablespoon caster sugar
over each half. Cook under a preheated hot grill for
3—4 minutes until golden. Put on a plate with 150 g
(5 oz) raspberries, drizzle with 2 tablespoons balsamic
vinegar and serve as a dessert.

walnut & blue cheese salad

Serves **4**
Preparation time **15 minutes**
Cooking time **5 minutes**

50 g (2 oz) **walnut halves**
2 tablespoons **icing sugar**
2 **chicory heads**
50 g (2 oz) **rocket**
1 **radicchio**, separated into
  leaves
125 g (4 oz) **blue cheese**,
  such as **Roquefort**

Dressing
1 teaspoon **Dijon mustard**
2 tablespoons **cider vinegar**
4 tablespoons **olive oil**

Put the walnuts in a plastic bag with the icing sugar and 1 tablespoon water and shake them until coated. Arrange the nuts on a baking sheet and roast in a preheated oven, 180°C (350°F), Gas Mark 4, for 5 minutes or until gold and crusted.

Separate the chicory leaves and put them into a large salad bowl with the rocket and radicchio. Crumble over the cheese and add the walnuts. Toss carefully.

Make the dressing by whisking together the mustard, vinegar and oil. Drizzle the dressing over the salad, mix lightly and serve.

For griddled radicchio & chicory salad, cut 2 chicory heads in half and 2 radicchio into quarters. Dust well with about 2 tablespoons icing sugar and place on an oiled griddle over medium heat. Griddle the chicory heads and radicchio until golden and caramelized. Combine 3 tablespoons cider vinegar and 4 tablespoons olive oil with 20 g (¾ oz) sultanas and heat in a small saucepan. Pour over the salad and combine well. Garnish with 3 tablespoons roughly chopped parsley and 125 g (4 oz) crumbled Gorgonzola cheese.

raspberry salad with toasties

Serves **4**

Preparation time **15 minutes**

Cooking time **4 minutes**

½ **red onion**, thinly sliced

125 g (4 oz) **mixed salad leaves**, including **baby red chard leaves**

100 g (3½ oz) fresh **raspberries**

2 tablespoons **balsamic vinegar**

1 **pomegranate**

8 slices, about 75 g (3 oz), **wholemeal French bread**

250 g (8 oz) **cottage cheese**

little **paprika**

Put the onion in a bowl with the salad leaves and raspberries. Drizzle over the vinegar and toss together.

Cut the pomegranate into quarters, flex the skin and pop out the seeds. Sprinkle half the seeds over the salad, then transfer the salad to 4 serving plates.

Toast the bread on both sides and arrange 2 slices in the centre of each serving plate. Spoon the cottage cheese on to the toast, sprinkle with the remaining pomegranate seeds and a little paprika and serve.

For raspberry salad dressing, to serve with the above salad, put 100 g (3½ oz) raspberries, 100 (3½ fl oz) raspberry vinegar, 150 ml (¼ pint) olive oil, 1 teaspoon caster sugar, 1 teaspoon Dijon mustard, 2 tablespoons chopped tarragon and 1 chopped garlic clove in a food processor or blender. Whiz until smooth, then taste and adjust the seasoning with salt and pepper. If you would like the dressing really smooth pour it through a fine sieve. It will keep, covered, for up to 7 days in the refrigerator.

chop salad, mexican style

Serves **4**
Preparation time **10 minutes**

1 **iceberg lettuce**
410 g (13½ oz) can **red
  kidney beans**, drained
  and rinsed
1 **avocado**, peeled, stoned
  and diced
2 ripe **tomatoes**, chopped
½ **red onion**, finely diced
1 tablespoon chopped
  coriander leaves
1 **jalapeño chilli** (optional),
  finely sliced
corn chips, to garnish
soured cream (optional),
  to serve

Dressing
juice of 1½ **limes**
3 tablespoons **olive oil**

Cut the lettuce into bite-sized pieces and put them into a large salad bowl. Add the beans, avocado, tomatoes and onion with the coriander and chilli (if used). Mix all the ingredients together.

Make the dressing by whisking together the lime juice and oil. Drizzle the dressing over the salad and mix lightly to combine. Garnish with lightly crushed corn chips and serve with soured cream (if liked).

For cranberry & chicken chop salad, roughly chop 2 cos lettuces and put the pieces into a large salad bowl. Shred 3 poached chicken breasts, each about 150 g (5 oz), and add to the lettuce with 60 g (2¼ oz) toasted pecan nuts, 50 g (2 oz) dried cranberries, 1 diced red apple and 1 cored, deseeded and chopped green pepper. Whisk 2 tablespoons apple cider vinegar and 4 tablespoons olive oil and season to taste with salt and pepper. Drizzle the dressing over the salad and lightly toss to combine. Garnish with crushed plain corn chips and serve.

tomato & mozzarella salad

Serves **4—6**
Preparation time **15 minutes**

500 g (1 lb) ripe **tomatoes**,
  preferably different types,
  such as **heirloom** and
  cherry and **plum**
about 3 tablespoons **olive oil**
2 tablespoons **aged balsamic
  vinegar**
small handful of **basil leaves**
150 g (5 oz) **mini mozzarella
  balls**
salt and **pepper**

Cut half the tomatoes into thick slices and the other half into wedges. Arrange the slices on a large serving plate, slightly overlapping each other.

Put the tomato wedges into a bowl and drizzle with olive oil and balsamic vinegar. Season to taste with salt and pepper. Mix carefully and arrange on top of the tomato slices.

Add the basil leaves and mozzarella balls to the tomato wedges. Drizzle the salad with more olive oil and balsamic vinegar, season to taste with salt and pepper and serve.

For tomato & pasta salad, cook 250 g (8 oz) fusilli or penne until it is just tender. Refresh in cold water. Chop 500 g (1 lb) tomatoes into chunks and stir through the still warm pasta, coat with olive oil and season to taste with salt and pepper. Mix through a large handful of torn basil leaves, garnish with Parmesan cheese shavings and serve.

big salads

thai-style beef salad

Serves **4–6**
Preparation time **20 minutes**
Cooking time **10 minutes**

125 g (4 oz) **green papaya**,
   peeled and deseeded
125 g (4 oz) **green mango**,
   peeled and stoned
handful of **mint leaves**
handful of **Thai basil leaves**
2 small, **elongated shallots**
1 tablespoon **vegetable oil**
4 **sirloin steaks**, each about
   125 g (4 oz)

Dressing
½ **chilli**, deseeded
1 cm (½ inch) **fresh root
   ginger**, peeled and finely
   sliced
1½ tablespoons **palm sugar**
juice of 2 **limes**
2 tablespoons **Thai fish
   sauce** (nam pla)

Finely grate or slice the papaya and mango into long, thin strips. Combine the mint and basil leaves in a large salad bowl with the mango and papaya. Finely slice the shallots and add them to the mixture.

Make the dressing. Crush the chilli with the ginger and sugar using a pestle and mortar. Add the lime juice and fish sauce to taste.

Heat a griddle pan on a high heat, add the oil and fry the steak for 5 minutes on each side. Remove the steak from the pan and leave it to rest for 5 minutes.

Thinly slice the steak diagonally and arrange neatly on the serving plates. Add the dressing to the salad, mix well to combine and serve with the steak.

For toasted rice khao koor, a special garnish you can add to this salad, put 3 tablespoons raw jasmine rice in a small frying pan over a medium heat and continue stirring until all the rice is golden in colour. Allow the rice to cool, then grind it coarsely in a spice grinder or using a pestle and mortar, and sprinkle over the finished salad.

spiced chicken & mango salad

Serves **4**
Preparation time **15 minutes**
Cooking time **5 minutes**

4 boneless, skinless **chicken breasts**, about 150 g (5 oz) each
6 teaspoons **mild curry paste**
4 tablespoons **lemon juice**
150 ml (¼ pint) **natural yogurt**
1 **mango**, peeled, stoned and cut into chunks
50 g (2 oz) **watercress**
½ **cucumber**, diced
½ **red onion**, finely chopped
½ **iceberg lettuce**

Cut the chicken breasts into long, thin slices. Put 4 teaspoons of the curry paste in a plastic bag with the lemon juice and mix together by squeezing the bag. Add the chicken and toss together.

Half-fill the base of a steamer with water and bring to the boil. Steam the chicken in a single layer, covered, for 5 minutes until cooked. Test with a knife or metal skewer; the juices will run clear when it is done.

Meanwhile, mix the remaining curry paste in a bowl with the yogurt.

Tear the watercress into bite-sized pieces. Add it to the yogurt dressing with the cucumber, red onion and mango and toss gently.

Tear the lettuce into pieces and arrange on 4 plates. Spoon the mango mixture over the top, add the warm chicken strips and serve immediately.

For chilli prawn, mango & avocado salad, replace the chicken with 400 g (13 oz) peeled, raw tiger prawns with the tails on. Prepare the salad in the same way as above but add the diced flesh of an avocado. Heat 2 tablespoons vegetable or groundnut oil in a nonstick frying pan over a high heat, and fry 1 finely chopped red chilli for 1 minute, then add the prawns and 2 finely chopped garlic cloves. Fry for 2 minutes until the prawns are pink and just cooked through. Mix through the salad and serve immediately.

japanese beef & noodle salad

Serves **4**
Preparation time **15 minutes**,
   plus marinating
Cooking time **15 minutes**

2 **sirloin steaks**, each about
   250 g (8 oz)
150 g (5 oz) **soba noodles**
1 small **daikon**, peeled and
   finely sliced
2 **carrots**, peeled and finely
   sliced
½ **cucumber**, peeled and finely
   sliced

Dressing
1 **garlic clove**, finely chopped
2 cm (¾ inch) **fresh root
   ginger**, peeled and chopped
5 tablespoons **soy sauce**
4 tablespoons **sweet chilli
   sauce**
5 teaspoons **sesame oil**

To garnish
5 **spring onions**, finely sliced
2 tablespoons **toasted
   sesame seeds**

Make the dressing. Mix the garlic and ginger with the soy sauce, sweet chilli sauce and sesame oil. Put the steaks in a non-metallic dish and add 2 tablespoons of the dressing, reserving the rest. Cover and leave to marinate for at least 2 hours, or preferably overnight.

Bring a saucepan of lightly salted water to the boil and cook the noodles for about 5 minutes or until done. Refresh in cold water, drain and transfer to a bowl.

Add the vegetables to the bowl with the noodles.

Heat a griddle pan on a high heat and cook the steaks for 5 minutes on each side until medium rare (longer if you prefer your meat well done). Allow to rest for 5 minutes and then finely slice. Drizzle the dressing over the noodle and vegetable mixture, add the sliced steak and combine well. Garnish with spring onions and toasted sesame seeds and serve immediately.

For sesame-crusted salmon & soba noodle salad,

combine 1 tablespoon black sesame seeds, 1 tablespoon white sesame seeds and 1 tablespoon coriander seeds. Put 4 small fillets of salmon, each about 125 g (4 oz), flesh side down into the seed mix and press the seeds on to the flesh. Heat 1 tablespoon vegetable oil in a large frying pan over a medium heat and fry the salmon, flesh side down, for 1 minute. Turn over the salmon and fry for about 4 minutes or until the salmon is just cooked through. Serve with the noodle salad as above, garnished with coriander leaves.

italian broccoli & egg salad

Serves **4**
Preparation time **10 minutes**
Cooking time **8 minutes**

4 eggs
300 g (10 oz) **broccoli**
2 small **leeks**, about 300 g
  (10 oz) in total
sprigs of **tarragon**, to garnish
  (optional)

Dressing
4 tablespoons **lemon juice**
2 tablespoons **olive oil**
2 teaspoons **clear honey**
1 tablespoon **capers**, drained
2 tablespoons chopped
  tarragon
salt and **pepper**

Half-fill the base of a steamer with water, add the eggs and bring to the boil. Cover with the steamer top and simmer for 8 minutes or until hard-boiled.

Meanwhile, cut the broccoli into florets and thickly slice the stems. Trim, slit and wash the leeks and cut them into thick slices. Add the broccoli to the top of the steamer and cook for 3 minutes, then add the leeks and cook for a further 2 minutes.

Make the dressing by mixing together the lemon juice, oil, honey, capers and tarragon in a salad bowl. Season to taste with salt and pepper.

Crack the eggs, cool them quickly under cold running water and remove the shells. Roughly chop the eggs.

Add the broccoli and leeks to the dressing, toss together and add the chopped eggs. Garnish with sprigs of tarragon (if liked) and serve warm with thickly sliced wholemeal bread.

For broccoli, bacon & pine nut salad, cut 125 g (4 oz) pancetta into pieces about 5 mm–3 cm (¼–1¼ inches). Heat a pan and dry-fry the pancetta until golden and crispy, then drain on kitchen paper. Toast 4 tablespoons pine nuts in a dry pan over a low heat until golden and toasted. Mix the pancetta with the broccoli and leeks, make a dressing as above and serve sprinkled with the pine nuts instead of the eggs.

bang bang chicken salad

Serves **4**
Preparation time **15 minutes**
Cooking time **10 minutes**

50 g (2 oz) **dried vermicelli noodles**
¼ **Savoy cabbage**, finely shredded
1 **carrot**, finely chopped
½ **cucumber**, finely chopped
juice of 1 **lime**
100 g (3½ oz) **peanut butter**
3 tablespoons **sweet chilli sauce**
1 tablespoon **soy sauce**
1 teaspoon **Chinese vinegar**
2 tablespoons **sesame oil**
2 tablespoons **vegetable oil**
3 poached **chicken breasts**, each about 150 g (5 oz)
3 finely sliced **spring onions**, to garnish

Bring a large saucepan of water to the boil and cook the noodles for 2 minutes. Refresh in cold water, drain and transfer to a large salad bowl.

Add the cabbage, carrot, cucumber and lime juice to the noodles.

Gently warm the peanut butter in a small saucepan. Add the sweet chilli sauce, soy sauce, vinegar and sesame and vegetable oils and whisk to a pouring consistency. (If necessary, add a little warm water to achieve the correct consistency.) Set the sauce aside to cool slightly.

Shred the chicken breasts, add the meat to the noodle mix and combine well. Arrange on serving plates, spoon over the peanut sauce and garnish with finely sliced spring onions.

For spicy beef skewers with noodle salad, cut 800 g (1 lb 10 oz) rump steak into 2 cm (¾ inch) squares. Mix together 1 tablespoon each ground ginger, chopped coriander and crushed cumin seeds with 3 crushed garlic cloves, 1 teaspoon crushed dry chilli and about 50 ml (2 fl oz) olive oil. Cover the beef in the mixture and leave to marinate for at least 1 hour. Thread the beef on to metal or presoaked wooden skewers and cook on a barbecue or a preheated hot griddle pan for 3 minutes on each side until cooked through. Serve with the noodle salad and spoon over the dressing.

mango & smoked chicken salad

Serves **4**
Preparation time **15 minutes**

2 ripe **avocados**, halved,
 stoned and peeled
2 tablespoons **lemon juice**
1 small **mango**
handful of **watercress**
50 g (2 oz) **cooked beetroot**,
 finely sliced
175 g (6 oz) **smoked chicken**

Dressing
3 tablespoons **olive oil**
1 teaspoon **wholegrain
 mustard**
1 teaspoon **clear honey**
2 teaspoons **cider vinegar**
salt and **pepper**

Slice or dice the avocado flesh and put it in a shallow bowl with the lemon juice.

Cut the mango in half on either side of the central stone, peel away the skin and slice or dice the flesh.

Make the dressing. Whisk together the oil, mustard, honey and vinegar. Season to taste with salt and pepper. Remove the avocado from the lemon juice and mix the juice into the dressing.

Arrange the watercress and beetroot on 4 plates or in a salad bowl and add the avocado and mango. Drizzle the dressing over the salad and stir to combine. Thinly slice the chicken and top the salad with the meat. Serve immediately.

For smoked chicken, white bean & thyme salad,
rinse and drain 2 x 410 g (13½ oz) cans cannellini beans and mix with 250 g (8 oz) halved cherry tomatoes, 100 g (3½ oz) rocket, 60 g (2¼ oz) pitted green olives and 1 tablespoon chopped thyme. Make the dressing by whisking 1 teaspoon Dijon mustard, 2 tablespoons cider vinegar, 4 tablespoons olive oil and 1 tablespoon chopped thyme. Dress the salad and serve with 175 g (6 oz) thinly sliced smoked chicken.

duck, clementine & tatsoi salad

Serves **4–6**
Preparation time **20 minutes**
Cooking time **15 minutes**

3 **duck breasts**, each about
 225 g (7½ oz)
300 g (10 oz) **green beans**,
 trimmed
3 **clementines**, peeled and
 segmented
200 g (7 oz) **tatsoi** or **spinach**

Dressing
juice of 2 **clementines**
1 tablespoon **white wine
 vinegar**
4 tablespoons **olive oil**
salt and **pepper**

Put the duck breasts, skin side down, in a cold
ovenproof dish and cook over a medium heat for
6 minutes or until the skin has turned crisp and brown.
Turn them over and cook for a further 2 minutes.
Transfer the duck to a preheated oven, 180°C (350°F),
Gas Mark 4, and cook for 5 minutes until cooked
through. Remove the duck breasts from the oven, cover
with foil and leave to rest.

Meanwhile, blanch the green beans in lightly salted
boiling water for 2 minutes until cooked but still firm
and bright green. Drain and refresh in cold water.
Transfer the beans to a large salad bowl with the
clementine segments.

Make the dressing by whisking together the
clementine juice, vinegar and oil in a small bowl.
Season to taste with salt and pepper.

Add the tatsoi or spinach to the beans and
clementines, drizzle over the dressing and combine
well. Slice the duck meat, combine it with the salad
and serve immediately.

For orange & mustard dressing, an alternative
dressing for this salad, cut 2 oranges in half and
place them, flesh side down, on a hot griddle pan. Cook
until they are charred and golden. Squeeze the orange
juice into a small saucepan and reduce over a medium
heat for 5 minutes until slightly thickened. Whisk in
1 tablespoon wholegrain mustard and 4 tablespoons
olive oil. Allow to cool slightly and serve warm.

prickly pear & prosciutto salad

Serves **4**
Preparation time **15 minutes**

4 **prickly pears**
125 g (4 oz) **haloumi cheese**
4 slices of **prosciutto**
50 g (2 oz) **watercress** or
  mizuna leaves
1 large **red chilli**, deseeded
  and finely chopped
2 tablespoons **lime juice**
2 tablespoons **pitted black
  olives**
handful of **chervil** sprigs
salt and **pepper**

Dressing
2 tablespoons **olive oil**
1 tablespoon **orange juice**
1 tablespoon **sherry vinegar**
pinch of **crushed chilli**

Wearing plastic gloves, cut each of the prickly pears in half and then into quarters. Remove the skins if preferred, taking care with the small, hairy spikes.

Thickly slice the haloumi and put one quarter in the centre of each serving plate. Arrange the prosciutto and prickly pear on top of the haloumi with the watercress or mizuna. Sprinkle the chilli over the plates with salt and pepper and the lime juice. Scatter olives around the plate and add the chervil.

Make the dressing by mixing the oil, orange juice, vinegar and crushed chilli. Just before serving, drizzle a little of the dressing over the salad and serve at once.

For pear, bresaola & dolcelatte salad, arrange about 400 g (13 oz) thinly sliced bresaola on a large serving plate so that the slices are slightly overlapping. Finely slice 2 pears and toss with 150 g (5 oz) rocket. Arrange the pears and rocket on the bresaola and drizzle with balsamic vinegar and olive oil. Crumble over 100 g (3½ oz) of dolcelatte cheese and serve.

prawn, mango & avocado salad

Serves **4**
Preparation time **10 minutes**

1 large **mango**, about 475 g
   (15 oz), peeled and stoned
1 ripe **avocado**, about 400 g
   (13 oz), peeled and stoned
2 large **cos lettuces**
16 large **cooked king
   prawns**, peeled but tails
   left on

Dressing
juice of 2 **limes**
1 teaspoon **palm sugar**
2 tablespoon **vegetable oil**
½ **chilli**, deseeded and finely
   chopped

Cut the mango and avocado flesh into 2 cm (¾ inch) pieces. Discard the outer layer of leaves and cut the stems off the lettuces, leaving the hearts. Separate the leaves and add them to the mango and avocado with the prawns.

Make the dressing by whisking together the lime juice, sugar and oil with the chilli. Add the dressing to the salad, toss carefully to mix and serve immediately.

For creamy mayonnaise dressing, a more luxurious accompaniment for this salad, mix 3 tablespoons Mayonnaise (see page 12), 2 tablespoons double cream, 2 teaspoons tomato sauce, 1½ teaspoons Worcestershire sauce, 2–3 drops Tabasco sauce, 1 tablespoon lemon juice and 1 tablespoon brandy. Season to taste with salt and pepper. Spoon the dressing over the salad or put a spoonful on the side of each plate as a dip for the prawns.

sesame-crusted salmon salad

Serves **4**

Preparation time **25 minutes**

Cooking time **4–10 minutes**

4 **spring onions**

2 **egg whites**

1 tablespoon **white sesame seeds**

1 tablespoon **black sesame seeds**

500 g (1 lb) **salmon fillet**

1 **frisée (curly-leaved endive)**, divided into leaves

2 bunches of **watercress**

salt and **pepper**

Dressing

3 tablespoons **white wine vinegar**

5 tablespoons **vegetable oil**

1 tablespoon **sesame oil**

1 tablespoon **soy sauce**

1 teaspoon **caster sugar**

1 bunch of **chives**, finely chopped

Cut the spring onions into thin strips and put them in cold water.

Lightly beat the egg whites. Mix the white and black sesame seeds with salt and pepper on a large plate. Dip the salmon fillet in the egg whites then roll it in the sesame seeds. Pat the salmon on the seeds all over to give a good, even coating. Heat a griddle pan, add the salmon and cook for 2 minutes each side for rare or 5 minutes for well done.

Make the dressing by mixing together the vinegar, oils, soy sauce, caster sugar and chives. Toss the frisée leaves and watercress in the dressing. Arrange the leaves on a large serving dish.

Finely slice the salmon fillet and place on top of the salad. Drain the spring onion curls, dry them on kitchen paper and sprinkle over the salmon. Serve immediately.

For sashimi salmon salad, grate 1 raw beetroot and 2 carrots and mix with 100 g (3½ oz) rocket. Make the dressing as above. Mix together 1 tablespoon each white and black sesame seeds. Slice as thinly as possible 2 skinless fillets of fresh salmon, each 150 g (5 oz), and arrange on individual plates. Drizzle the dressing over the salad, garnish with the sesame seeds and serve with the salmon.

pork larb

Serves **4**
Preparation time **15 minutes**
Cooking time **15 minutes**

1 tablespoon **groundnut oil**
2 cm (¾ inch) **fresh root ginger**, peeled and finely chopped
2 **lemon grass**, white stems chopped
3 **kaffir lime leaves**, finely sliced
600 g (1¼ lb) **minced pork**
2 tablespoons **Thai fish sauce** (nam pla)
juice of 1½ limes
½ **cucumber**
1 **iceberg lettuce**

To garnish
30 g (1¼ oz) **roasted peanuts**, chopped
small bunch of **mint**, finely chopped
small bunch of **coriander**, finely chopped
1 **red chilli**, deseeded and finely chopped

Heat the oil in a large, nonstick frying pan or wok over a high heat, add the ginger, chilli, lemon grass and lime leaves and fry for 1 minute.

Add the pork and stir-fry for 4—5 minutes until slightly browned and cooked through. Add the fish sauce and lime juice to taste then remove the pan from the heat.

Cut the cucumber into very fine strands and arrange on serving plates next to a lettuce leaf. Serve the pork on the lettuce, garnished with the chopped peanuts, herbs and red chilli.

For sang choy bow, instead of cutting the iceberg lettuce into wedges break the leaves into cup shapes. Cook the pork in the same way as above and spoon the mixture into the lettuce leaf cups. Garnish with 30 g (1¼ oz) chopped peanuts and mint and coriander leaves and serve immediately.

peanut, squid & noodle salad

Serves **4**
Preparation time **25 minutes**,
  plus standing
Cooking time **15 minutes**

175 g (6 oz) **thin rice
  noodles**
500 g (1 lb) prepared **baby
  squid**
3 **red chillies**, deseeded and
  finely chopped
3 **garlic cloves**, crushed
2 tablespoons chopped
  coriander, plus extra leaves
  to serve
3 tablespoons **groundnut oil**
175 g (6 oz) **peanuts**
125 g (4 oz) **green beans**,
  shredded
3 tablespoons **Thai fish
  sauce** (nam pla)
1 teaspoon **caster sugar**
3 tablespoons **lemon juice**
thick **lime wedges**, to serve
  (optional)

Soak the noodles in boiling water for 5–8 minutes or
until they are soft. Drain well and rinse in cold water.

Cut the squid bodies in half lengthways and make a
series of slashes in a diagonal criss-cross pattern on
the underside of each piece of squid.

Mix the chillies with the garlic and coriander. Toss with
the squid pieces, then leave to stand for 20 minutes.

Heat the oil in a wok and toast the peanuts for 2–3
minutes until golden brown. Remove from the oil and
reserve. Add the squid to the oil and quickly stir-fry for
2–3 minutes or until they have begun to curl and turn
white. Set aside with the peanuts.

Stir-fry the beans for 2 minutes. Mix the fish sauce,
sugar, lemon juice and 3 tablespoons water and cook
for a further 1 minute. Remove the pan from the heat,
add the drained noodles and toss together. Add the
peanuts, squid and coriander leaves and toss again.
Serve warm or cool with thick lime wedges (if used).

For sweet chilli & lime chicken, prepare the noodle
salad as above but omit the squid and add the chilli,
garlic and coriander to the salad at the end, when
tossing. Mix 3 tablespoons sweet chilli sauce and the
rind and juice of 1 lime. Brush 4 chicken breasts, each
about 150 g (5 oz), with some of the mixture. Put the
chicken, skin side up, on a foil-lined baking sheet and
cook under a preheated hot grill for 8–10 minutes.
Brush the chicken again with more of the mixture and
cook for 5 minutes until crispy and cooked through.
Slice the chicken and serve on top of the salad.

marinated tofu & mushroom salad

Serves **4**

Preparation time **15 minutes**, plus marinating

Cooking time **5 minutes**

250 g (8 oz) **firm tofu**

500 g (1 lb) **mushrooms**, including **enoki, shiitake, wood ear** and **oyster**

Marinade

1 **garlic clove**, finely chopped

2 cm (¾ inch) **fresh root ginger**, peeled and finely sliced

5 tablespoons **soy sauce**

1 tablespoon **mirin**

2 tablespoons **sweet chilli sauce**

1½ tablespoons **sesame oil**

2 **star anise**

To garnish

5 **spring onions**, finely sliced

2 tablespoons **toasted sesame seeds**

Make the marinade. Mix the garlic and ginger with the soy sauce, mirin, sweet chilli sauce and oil. Add the star anise. Put the tofu in a non-metallic dish, pour over the marinade, cover and refrigerate for at least 2 hours or overnight if possible.

Cut the mushrooms into bite-sized pieces and sauté in a hot saucepan for 1 minute. Cut the marinated tofu into 2 cm (¾ inch) squares, mix with the mushrooms and pour over the remaining marinade. Garnish with finely sliced spring onions and sesame seeds and serve immediately.

For tofu & rice salad, cook 200 g (7 oz) sushi rice according to the instructions on the packet. While the rice is still warm season it with 100–150 ml (3½–5 fl oz) sushi pickle. Cut 500 g (1 lb) mixed mushrooms into bite-sized pieces and cook briefly, then mix though the rice with 1 carrot cut into julienne strips and a small bunch of finely sliced spring onions. Mix the salad well, garnish with finely sliced deep-fried bean curd and toasted sesame seeds and serve immediately.

duck, hazelnut & peach salad

Serves **4**
Preparation time **15 minutes**
Cooking time **20 minutes**

3 **duck breasts**, each about
    200 g (7 oz)
4 **peaches**
60 g (2¼ oz) **toasted
    hazelnuts**, roughly chopped
125 g (4 oz) **rocket**

Dressing
1 teaspoon **Dijon mustard**
2 tablespoon **balsamic
    vinegar**
4 tablespoons **hazelnut oil**
salt and **pepper**

Heat a griddle pan until it is very hot and fry the duck, skin side down, for 4 minutes or until golden brown. Turn the duck over and cook for 2 minutes, then transfer it to a preheated oven, 190°C (375°F), Gas Mark 5, and cook for 6–8 minutes until cooked through. Remove from the oven, cover with foil and leave to rest.

Meanwhile, halve the peaches and remove the stones. Heat a griddle pan to a medium heat, add the peach halves, cut side down, and cook until they are golden yellow. Cut the peaches into wedges and mix them in a bowl with the hazelnuts and rocket.

Make the dressing by whisking together the mustard, vinegar and oil. Season to taste with salt and pepper.

Thinly slice the duck meat and add it to the salad. Drizzle over the dressing, combine gently and serve.

For duck, asparagus & hazelnut salad, put 4 duck legs on a baking sheet and season with salt and pepper. Roast the duck legs in a preheated oven, 160°C (325°F), Gas Mark 3, for 45–60 minutes or until cooked through but not dry. Remove the woody ends from a large bunch of asparagus and transfer the spears to a baking sheet. Cook under a preheated hot grill for 3–4 minutes, turning occasionally. Remove the asparagus from the grill and place in a bowl with 60 g (2¼ oz) roughly chopped roasted hazelnuts and 125 g (4 oz) rocket. Pour over the dressing as above and stir to combine. Serve with the duck.

quail, plum & cashew nut salad

Serves **4**

Preparation time **20 minutes**

Cooking time **12 minutes**

4 **quails**, butterflied

2 tablespoons **Plum Sauce** (see page 15)

4 **plums**, quartered and stoned

100 g (3½ oz) **lamb's lettuce**

50 g (2 oz) **toasted cashew nuts**

Dressing

1 **red chilli**

1½ tablespoons **plum sauce**

juice of 1½ **limes**

2 tablespoons **sunflower oil**

Put the quails in a foil-lined baking tin and brush each with some plum sauce. Cook under a preheated hot grill for 5–6 minutes on each side until golden and just cooked through. Cut each quail into 4 equal sections and place them in a large salad bowl.

Meanwhile, make the dressing by mixing together the chilli, plum sauce, lime juice and oil.

Put the plums, lamb's lettuce and cashew nuts in the bowl with the quail pieces. Add the dressing, toss lightly to combine and serve immediately.

For crispy soy quail & pear salad, deseed and finely chop 1 red chilli and mix it in a bowl with 100 ml (3½ fl oz) soy sauce, 2 tablespoons brown sugar and the juice and rind of 1 orange. Peel and roughly chop 1 cm (½ inch) fresh root ginger and add to the bowl with 1 star anise. Marinate 4 butterflied quails in the mixture overnight. Slice 2 pears and place them in a large salad bowl with 100 g (3½ oz) lamb's lettuce and 1 finely sliced red pepper. Remove the quail from the marinade, arrange them on a foil-lined baking sheet and cook under a preheated hot grill for 4 minutes on each side until cooked and crispy. Season with salt and pepper. Toss the salad with the same dressing as above and serve garnished with 50 g (2 oz) toasted cashew nuts.

chicken & asparagus salad

Serves **2**
Preparation time **10 minutes**
Cooking time **5 minutes**

150 g (5 oz) **asparagus**, cut
 into 5 cm (2 inch) lengths
200 g (7 oz) **smoked chicken
 breast**
125 g (4 oz) **cherry
 tomatoes**, halved
300 g (10 oz) can **cannellini
 beans**, drained and rinsed
handful of **chives**, chopped

Dressing
2 tablespoons **olive oil**
2 teaspoons **clear honey**
2 teaspoons **balsamic
 vinegar**
2 teaspoons **wholegrain
 mustard**
1 **garlic clove**

Cook the asparagus in a large saucepan of lightly
salted boiling water for about 4 minutes or until just
tender. Drain and plunge into cold water to prevent
further cooking. Pat dry with kitchen paper.

Cut the chicken into bite-sized pieces and transfer
them to a large salad bowl. Add the tomatoes, beans,
asparagus and chopped chives and mix well.

Make the dressing by whisking the oil, honey, vinegar
and mustard with the crushed garlic in a small bowl.
Pour the dressing over the salad and toss well to coat.

For chicken, asparagus & haloumi salad, prepare
150 g (5 oz) asparagus as above and set aside. Heat
a griddle pan and cook 4 chicken breasts, each about
150 g (5 oz), for 5–6 minutes on each side or until
cooked. Set aside, cover with foil and keep warm. Cut
250 g (8 oz) haloumi cheese into 5 mm (¼ inch) slices
and fry for 2 minutes on each side until golden and
crispy. Mix 1 teaspoon Dijon mustard, 3 tablespoons
lemon juice, 4 tablespoons olive oil and 2 tablespoons
roughly chopped tarragon in a small bowl. Slice
the chicken and arrange on serving plates with the
haloumi and asparagus. Drizzle over the dressing
and serve.

duck & soya bean salad

Serves **4**
Preparation time **10 minutes**

500 g (1 lb) **Peking duck**
200 g (7 oz) cooked **soya
    beans**
1 **cucumber**, finely sliced
5 **spring onions**, very finely
    sliced, plus extra to garnish
Sichuan pepper, to garnish

Dressing
2 tablespoons **hoisin sauce**
4 tablespoons **soy sauce**
juice of **1 lime**

Shred the duck and mix it with the soya beans,
cucumber and spring onions in a large salad bowl.

Make the dressing by whisking the hoisin and soy
sauces with the lime juice in a small bowl. Drizzle
the mixture over the duck salad and toss gently to
combine. Garnish with some spring onion and
a sprinkling of Sichuan pepper and serve at once.

For poached salmon & soya bean salad, blanch
300 g (10 oz) green beans, 200 g (7 oz) green
peas and 200 g (7 oz) soya beans in lightly salted
boiling water. Refresh in cold water and set aside.
Bring a saucepan of lightly salted water to the boil.
Put 3 boneless, skinless salmon fillets, each about
175 g (6 oz), into the water. Reduce the heat to a
rolling simmer and cook for 3–4 minutes until the
salmon is still pink in the middle. Remove them from
the water and leave to cool. Cut ½ cucumber into small
dice and mix with the blanched vegetables and 75 g
(3 oz) rocket. Flake the salmon into the vegetables.
Whisk 2 tablespoons sweet chilli sauce, 2 tablespoons
soya sauce and the juice of 1 lime. Drizzle the dressing
over the salad and serve immediately.

peanut, pomelo & prawn salad

Serves **4**
Preparation time **15 minutes**
Cooking time **1–2 minutes**

1 large **pomelo**
125 g (4 oz) **peanuts**, toasted
and roughly chopped
175 g (6 oz) **raw tiger
prawns**, peeled
4 **spring onions**
6 **mint leaves**
2 tablespoons **grapefruit
juice**
½ tablespoon **Thai fish sauce**
(nam pla)
1 large **red chilli**, deseeded
and finely sliced
pinch of **crushed chilli** or
black pepper
pinch of **grated nutmeg**
4–5 **frisée** (curly-leaved
endive) or **lollo rosso** leaves

Cut the pomelo in half and scoop out the segments
and juice. Discard the pith and thick skin surrounding
each segment and break the flesh into small pieces.
Stir the peanuts into the pomelo flesh. Set aside to
allow the flavours to blend.

Bring a saucepan of water to the boil and simmer the
prawns for 1–2 minutes or until they turn pink and are
cooked through. Remove them with a slotted spoon
and drain well.

Finely shred the spring onions and mint leaves. Add
the prawns to the pomelo flesh with the grapefruit
juice, fish sauce, spring onions and mint.

Sprinkle the red chilli, crushed chilli or pepper and
nutmeg over the salad and toss together. Line the
inside of a bowl with salad leaves and spoon in the
prawn and pomelo mixture. Serve immediately.

For pomelo & prawn salad with vermicelli noodles,
put 150 g (5 oz) vermicelli noodles into a large bowl
and cover with boiling hot water. Leave to stand for
5 minutes or until the noodles are cooked through.
Whisk the juice of 1 lime, 1 tablespoon sweet chilli
sauce and 1 teaspoon fish sauce. Drain the noodles
and pour the dressing over them. Toss well to
combine. Prepare the rest of the salad as above, but
omitting the salad leaves. Toss all the ingredients
together, garnish with peanuts and roughly chopped
herbs and serve immediately.

spicy lamb & couscous salad

Serves **4**
Preparation time **30 minutes**,
  plus marinating
Cooking time **15 minutes**

400 g (13 oz) **lamb**
2 teaspoons **ras el hanout**
3 tablespoons **vegetable oil**
200 g (7 oz) **couscous**
200 ml (7 fl oz) hot **chicken
  stock**
small bunch of **coriander**
2 **preserved lemons**
50 g (2 oz) ready-to-eat **dried
  apricots**, chopped
25 g (1 oz) **currants**
salt and **pepper**

Dressing
4 tablespoons **yogurt**
¼ teaspoon **ras el hanout**
1 tablespoon chopped
  coriander
2 tablespoons **lemon juice**

Cut the lamb into 2.5 cm (1 in) dice. Whisk together the ras el hanout and vegetable oil and marinate the lamb for at least 1 hour or overnight if possible.

Thread the meat on to metal or presoaked wooden skewers, putting about 6 pieces of lamb on each one.

Meanwhile, put the couscous in a bowl, add the hot chicken stock, cover and allow to stand. Chop the coriander, reserving some leaves for garnish. Remove and finely chop the peel from the preserved lemons and chop the apricots. Add the preserved lemon to the cooked couscous with the coriander, apricots and currants, season with salt and pepper and mix lightly.

Make the dressing by mixing all the ingredients in a small bowl. Set aside.

Cook the lamb skewers on a preheated hot griddle pan for 3–4 minutes each side until cooked through. Spoon the couscous on to serving plates and top each with 2–3 skewers and some yogurt dressing.

For vegetarian couscous salad, prepare the couscous as above, but using 200 ml (7 fl oz) hot vegetable stock. Halve 5 Thai aubergines lengthways, drizzle with olive oil and cook on a hot griddle. Set aside. Cut 2 courgettes into long ribbons and 1 small sweet potato into strips and griddle. Put all the vegetables in a baking tin, drizzle with olive oil, salt and pepper and cook in a preheated oven, 190°C (375°F), Gas Mark 5, for 15 minutes until tender. Serve the vegetables on the couscous with the yogurt dressing.

celery, artichoke & chicken salad

Serves **4—6**
Preparation time **15 minutes**
Cooking time **5 minutes**

6 thin slices of **rye bread**
2 tablespoons **olive oil**
1 leafy **celery head**
100 g (3½ oz) canned or
    bottled **artichoke hearts**,
    drained and grilled
2 tablespoons roughly
    chopped **parsley**
3 smoked **chicken breasts**,
    each about 100 g (3½ oz)
salt and **pepper**

Dressing
1 teaspoon **Dijon mustard**
2 tablespoons **white wine
    vinegar**
4 tablespoons **olive oil**

Arrange the rye bread slices on a baking sheet. Drizzle with olive oil, season with salt and pepper and bake in a preheated oven, 190°C (375°F), Gas Mark 5, for 5 minutes until crispy like croûtons. Remove from the oven and set aside.

Remove the leaves from the celery, reserving all the inside leaves. Finely slice 3 sticks and put them in a large salad bowl with the leaves, add the artichokes and parsley.

Thinly slice the smoked chicken breasts and add to the bowl with the celery and artichokes.

Make the dressing by whisking together the mustard, vinegar and oil. Drizzle over the salad and lightly mix.

Place a piece of rye toast on each serving plate and top with some salad.

For smoked chicken & cannellini bean salad,

rinse and drain 410 g (13½ oz) can of cannellini beans and put them in a large salad bowl. Add 75 g (3 oz) sun-blushed tomatoes, 100 g (3½ oz) blanched green beans, 100 g (3½ oz) grilled artichokes and 3 roughly chopped smoked chicken breasts, each about 100 g (3½ oz). In a small bowl whisk 1 tablespoon chopped parsley, 1 tablespoon chopped basil, 1 teaspoon chopped tarragon, 1 crushed garlic clove, 2 tablespoons chardonnay vinegar and 4 tablespoons olive oil. Season with salt and pepper. Toss the dressing through the salad and serve.

beef & cucumber salad

Serves **4**

Preparation time **15 minutes**, plus standing

Cooking time **12 minutes**

2 trimmed lean **rump** or **sirloin** steaks, each about 150 g (5 oz)

150 g (5 oz) **baby sweetcorn cobs**

1 large **cucumber**

1 small **red onion**, finely chopped

3 tablespoons chopped **coriander leaves**

4 tablespoons **rice wine vinegar**

4 tablespoons **sweet chilli dipping sauce**

2 tablespoons **sesame seeds**, to garnish

Put the steaks on a preheated hot griddle pan and cook for 3–4 minutes on each side. Allow to rest for 10–15 minutes then slice thinly.

Put the sweetcorn in a saucepan of boiling water and cook for 3–4 minutes or until tender. Refresh under cold water and drain well.

Slice the cucumber in half lengthways, then scoop out and discard the seeds using a small spoon. Cut the cucumber into 5 mm (¼ inch) slices.

Put the onion in a large salad bowl with the beef, sweetcorn, cucumber and chopped coriander. Stir in the rice wine vinegar and chilli sauce and mix well. Garnish the salad with lightly toasted sesame seeds and serve.

For beef salad with roasted shallots, peel about 20 shallots and put them on a baking sheet. Drizzle with olive oil and season with salt and pepper. Roast in a preheated oven, 190°C (375°F), Gas Mark 5, for 20 minutes until golden and soft. In a small bowl mix 1 teaspoon Dijon mustard, 2 tablespoons cabernet sauvignon vinegar, 1 tablespoon chopped thyme and 4 tablespoons olive oil. Cook the steaks as above and leave to rest, then finely slice and mix the meat with the roast shallots and 150 g (5 oz) watercress. Drizzle over the dressing and serve immediately.

pomelo, prawn & pork salad

Serves **4**
Preparation time **20 minutes**
Cooking time **10–15 minutes**

250 g (8 oz) **pork belly**
2 **pomelos**, peeled and
    segmented
200 g (7 oz) **peeled, cooked**
    king prawns
small bunch of **mint**,
    separated into leaves
small bunch of **coriander**,
    roughly chopped
small bunch of **Thai basil**,
    roughly chopped
3 tablespoons roughly
    chopped **roasted peanuts**,
    to garnish

Dressing
6 tablespoons **palm sugar**
juice of 2 **limes**
2 tablespoons **Thai fish
    sauce** (nam pla)
2 tablespoons **water**

Cut the pork belly into pieces about 2 cm–5 mm (¾–¼ inch). Heat a frying pan over a high heat and cook the pork for 4 minutes until golden and crispy, then drain on kitchen paper.

Make the dressing. Put the sugar in a small, heavy-based saucepan and cook for 4 minutes over a medium heat until the sugar is bubbling and has turned a deep caramel colour. Carefully, because it might spit, whisk in the lime juice, fish sauce and water. Remove from the heat and set aside to cool slightly.

Combine the pomelo segments, the prawns, the herbs and the cooked pork belly in a large salad bowl. Toss lightly and transfer the salad to serving plates. Drizzle the caramel dressing over the top, garnish with roasted peanuts and serve.

For pomelo, prawn, pork & shallot salad, add fried shallots to the above. You can buy these ready-prepared in Asian grocers or make your own. Heat 500 ml (17 fl oz) vegetable oil in a heavy-based frying pan or wok. Heat the oil to 160°C (325°F) and add 3 finely sliced shallots, stirring constantly to make sure they cook evenly. When they are golden, carefully remove them from the oil with a slotted spoon and drain on kitchen paper. Add to the salad above with the pomelo, prawns, pork and herbs.

warm
salads

roast tomato & asparagus salad

Serves **4**
Preparation time **20 minutes**
Cooking time **2 hours**

2 large **beefsteak tomatoes**
6 tablespoons **olive oil**
2 **garlic cloves**
4 sprigs of **thyme**
bunch of **wild garlic**, roughly
  chopped
½ bunch of **basil**, roughly
  chopped
1 tablespoon **white wine
  vinegar**
20 **asparagus spears**,
  trimmed
30 g (1¼ oz) **rocket**
grated **Parmesan cheese**,
  to serve
salt and **pepper**

Halve each tomato horizontally and put them, cut side up, on a baking sheet. Drizzle ½ teaspoon olive oil over each, season with salt and pepper, half a crushed garlic clove and a sprig of thyme. Cook in a preheated oven, 110°C (225°F), Gas Mark ¼, for at least 2 hours. The tomatoes should be slightly dehydrated but still juicy.

Whiz the wild garlic, basil and 5 tablespoons olive oil in a food processor. The garlic should still be slightly chunky. Place in a bowl and whisk in the vinegar. Season with salt and pepper.

Arrange the asparagus on a dish and drizzle over ½ tablespoon oil. Season with a little salt and pepper. Heat a griddle pan over a high heat and cook the asparagus for about 5 minutes, turning the spears every 1–2 minutes. They will be just tender in the middle. Return the asparagus to the dish, cover with clingfilm and leave to steam slightly.

Remove the tomatoes from the oven and arrange on serving plates. Top each tomato with 5 asparagus spears and a drizzle of the wild garlic dressing. Serve with the rocket and a sprinkling of Parmesan cheese.

For tomato & mozzarella pasta salad, cook 250 g (8 oz) penne until just tender, refresh in cold water, drizzle with olive oil and reserve. Chop 2 beefsteak tomatoes into chunks and stir through the pasta. Drizzle over olive oil and 2 tablespoons balsamic vinegar and salt and pepper. Mix through ½ bunch torn basil leaves and 2 mozzarella balls, each about 150 g (5 oz), torn into 2–3 pieces, and serve.

chickpea & pepper salad

Serves **4**

Preparation time **25 minutes**

Cooking time **35 minutes**

2 x 410 g (13½ oz) cans
  chickpeas

2 **red peppers**, cored,
  deseeded and halved

1 **yellow pepper**, cored,
  deseeded and halved

1 **red onion**, quartered but
  held together by the root

4 **plum tomatoes**, cut into
  wedges

olive oil

2 tablespoons **fennel seeds**

small bunch of **parsley**,
  chopped

salt and **pepper**

tzatziki (see below), to serve

Dressing

4 tablespoons **sherry vinegar**

3 tablespoons **olive oil**

1 **garlic clove**, crushed

½ teaspoon **ground cumin**

Rinse the chickpeas in cold water and leave to drain. Core and deseed the peppers and cut the flesh into 2 cm (¾ inch) strips. Cut the onion in half and then cut each half into quarters, leaving the root on so the wedges stay together

Drizzle the peppers, onions and tomatoes with olive oil and salt and pepper. Heat a griddle pan over a high heat and cook the peppers for 2 minutes on each side. Slice the peppers and place in an ovenproof dish and cook the onion in the same way. Place the onion and tomatoes with the peppers, sprinkle with fennel seeds and cook in a preheated oven, 180°C (350°F), Gas Mark 4, for 20 minutes until done.

Meanwhile, make the dressing. Whisk together the vinegar and oil with the crushed garlic and cumin.

Transfer the drained chickpeas to a large salad bowl and mix in the hot vegetables and chopped parsley. Season to taste with salt and pepper, drizzle over the dressing and stir to combine. Serve with a dollop of tzatziki, if liked (see below).

For tzatziki, to serve with the above salad, cut a cucumber in half lengthways and remove the seeds with a spoon. Finely dice the flesh and mix it with 250 ml (8 fl oz) Greek yogurt, 1 crushed garlic clove, 1 tablespoon olive oil, 2 tablespoons chopped mint and 1 tablespoon lemon juice. Season to taste with salt and pepper, cover and leave in the refrigerator for at least 1 hour before serving.

scallop, parsnip & carrot salad

Serves **4**
Preparation time **15 minutes**
Cooking time **30 minutes**

4 **carrots**, quartered
  lengthways
3 **parsnips**, quartered
  lengthways
2 tablespoons **olive oil**
1 tablespoon **cumin seeds**
12 fresh **king scallops**
2 tablespoons **lemon juice**
salt and **pepper**
chopped **parsley**, to garnish

Dressing
4 tablespoons **natural yogurt**
2 tablespoons **lemon juice**
2 tablespoons **olive oil**
1 teaspoon **ground cumin**

Put the carrots and parsnips on a foil-lined baking sheet. Drizzle with 1 tablespoon of the oil, scatter over the cumin seeds, season with salt and pepper and cook in a preheated oven, 180°C (350°F), Gas Mark 4, for 20–25 minutes.

Meanwhile, make the dressing. Mix the yogurt, lemon juice, oil and ground cumin in a small bowl. Season to taste with salt and pepper.

Trim the scallops to remove the tough muscle on the outside of the white fleshy part. Heat the remaining oil in a large frying pan and fry the scallops for 2 minutes on each side until they are just cooked through. Pour over the lemon juice and transfer the scallops and cooking juices to a large salad bowl.

Add the carrots and parsnips to the bowl and mix, then transfer them to a serving dish, spoon over the yogurt dressing, garnish with parsley and serve.

For curried scallops & carrot salad, roast 4 carrots and 3 parsnips as above but omit the cumin. Combine 1 tablespoon curry powder with 500 ml (17 fl oz) milk and 60 g (2¼ oz) butter. Soften 2 tablespoons cornflour with a little of the milk and whisk to combine. Transfer the mixture to a small, heavy-based saucepan and bring to the boil, whisking all the time so that lumps do not form. When you have a smooth, thickened sauce drop in the scallops and cook them for 3 minutes. Transfer the carrots and parsnips to a serving plate, arrange the scallops on top and serve with the sauce.

asian salmon salad

Serves **4**
Preparation time **20 minutes**
Cooking time **8–10 minutes**

150 g (5 oz) **long-grain rice**
4 **salmon fillets**, each about
   125 g (4 oz)
3 tablespoons **tamari sauce**
100 g (3½ oz) **sugar snap**
   peas, halved lengthways
1 large **carrot**, cut into
   matchsticks
4 **spring onions**, thinly sliced
100 g (3½ oz) **bean sprouts**
6 teaspoons **sunflower oil**
3 tablespoons **sesame seeds**
2 teaspoons **Thai fish sauce**
   (nam pla) (optional)
2 teaspoons **rice vinegar** or
   white wine vinegar
small bunch of **coriander** or
   basil, leaves roughly torn

Half-fill a saucepan with water and bring to the boil. Add the rice and simmer for 8 minutes.

Meanwhile, put the salmon on a foil-lined grill rack and drizzle over 1 tablespoon of the tamari sauce. Cook under a preheated grill for 8–10 minutes, turning once, until the fish is browned and flakes easily.

Add the sugar snap peas to the rice and cook for 1 minute. Drain, rinse with cold water and drain again. Tip into a salad bowl. Add the carrot, spring onions and bean sprouts to the salad bowl.

Heat 1 teaspoon of the oil in a nonstick frying pan, add the sesame seeds and fry until just beginning to brown. Add 1 tablespoon tamari sauce and quickly cover the pan so that the seeds do not ping out. Remove the pan from the heat and leave to stand for 1–2 minutes, then mix in the remaining tamari sauce, oil, fish sauce (if used) and vinegar.

Add the sesame mixture to the salad and toss together. Take the skin off the salmon and flake into pieces, discarding any bones. Add to the salad with the torn herb leaves and serve immediately.

For Asian tofu salad, cut 250 g (8 oz) firm tofu into 5 mm (¼ inch) slices. Mix 2 tablespoons soy sauce, 1 tablespoon sweet chilli sauce and 1 teaspoon sesame oil and marinate the tofu for at least 1 hour. Prepare the salad as above but omit the salmon. When the salad is ready, heat a nonstick frying pan and fry the tofu for 2–3 minutes on each side. Serve on top of the salad with any remaining marinade.

chorizo, pepper & oregano salad

Serves **2–4**
Preparation time **15 minutes**
Cooking time **15 minutes**

1 **red onion**
2 **red peppers**
2 **yellow peppers**
200 g (7 oz) **chorizo sausage**
1 tablespoon **olive oil**
2 tablespoons **sherry vinegar**
½ bunch of **oregano**, roughly
   chopped
75 g (3 oz) **rocket**
salt and **pepper**
romesco sauce (see below),
   to serve

Finely dice the red onion. Core and deseed the peppers and cut the flesh into 2 cm (¾ inch) squares. Slice the chorizo.

Heat the oil in a large frying pan over a high heat and cook the peppers for 2–3 minutes until they start to colour. Add the chorizo and fry for another 3 minutes, then reduce the heat to low and add the onion. Cook for a further 3 minutes. Deglaze the pan with the sherry vinegar and reduce for 1 minute.

Transfer the contents of the pan to a large salad bowl and leave to cool slightly, then toss with the oregano and rocket. Season with salt and pepper and serve with romesco sauce.

For romesco sauce, to serve with the above salad, soak 1 dried anchero chilli in water for 1 hour, then drain. Put 4 ready-marinated red peppers, the anchero chilli, 2 peeled and deseeded tomatoes, 20 g (¾ oz) blanched toasted almonds and 20 g (¾ oz) roasted hazelnuts, 1 garlic clove, 1 tablespoon red wine vinegar and 1 teaspoon smoked paprika into a food processor or blender and whiz briefly to make a smooth sauce. Season to taste with salt and pepper and serve with the salad.

chicken couscous salad

Serves **4**

Preparation time **20 minutes**,
plus marinating

Cooking time **20 minutes**

4 boneless, skinless **chicken
breasts**, each about 125 g
(4 oz)

300 g (10 oz) **couscous**

300 ml (½ pint) hot **chicken
stock**

1 **pomegranate**

rind and **juice** of 1 **orange**

small bunch of **coriander**

small bunch of **mint**

Marinade

1½ tablespoons **curry paste
(tikka masala)**

5 tablespoons **natural yogurt**

1 teaspoon **olive oil**

2 tablespoons **lemon juice**

Make a marinade by mixing the curry paste, yogurt and oil. Put the chicken in a non-metallic dish, cover with half the marinade and leave for at least 1 hour.

Put the couscous in a bowl, add the hot stock, cover and leave for 8 minutes.

Meanwhile, cut the pomegranate in half and remove the seeds. Add them to the couscous with the orange rind and juice.

Remove the chicken from the marinade, reserving the marinade, and transfer to a foil-lined baking sheet. Cook in a preheated oven, 190°C (375°F), Gas Mark 5, for 6–7 minutes, then transfer to a preheated hot grill and cook for 2 minutes until caramelized. Cover with foil and leave to rest for 5 minutes.

Roughly chop the coriander and mint, reserving some whole coriander leaves for garnish, and add to the couscous. Thinly slice the chicken. Spoon the couscous on to plates and add the chicken. Thin the reserved marinade with the lemon juice and drizzle over the couscous. Garnish with the reserved coriander leaves and serve immediately.

For pomegranate vinaigrette, an alternative dressing for this salad, whisk together 150 ml (¼ pint) pomegranate juice, 2 tablespoons pomegranate molasses (available from Middle Eastern stores and some supermarkets), 2 tablespoons red wine vinegar and 3 tablespoons olive oil.

pumpkin, feta & pine nut salad

Serves **4**
Preparation time **20 minutes**
Cooking time
   about **25 minutes**

500 g (1 lb) **pumpkin**
olive oil
2 sprigs of **thyme**, roughly
   chopped
200 g (7 oz) **mixed baby
   salad leaves**
50 g (2 oz) **feta cheese**
salt and **pepper**
2 tablespoons **toasted pine
   nuts**, to garnish

Dressing
1 teaspoon **Dijon mustard**
2 tablespoons **balsamic
   vinegar**
4 tablespoons **olive oil**

Skin and deseed the pumpkin, cut the flesh into 2 cm (¾ inch) squares and put them in a roasting tin. Drizzle with olive oil, scatter over the thyme and season with salt and pepper. Roast the pumpkin in a preheated oven, 190°C (375°F), Gas Mark 5, for 25 minutes or until cooked though. Remove the pumpkin from the oven and allow to cool slightly.

Meanwhile, make the dressing. Whisk together the mustard, vinegar and oil and set aside.

Put the mixed leaves in a large salad bowl, add the cooked pumpkin and crumble in the feta. Drizzle over the dressing and toss carefully to combine. Transfer the mixture to serving plates, garnish with toasted pine nuts and serve immediately.

For roast pumpkin, bacon, sage & pasta salad, prepare the pumpkin as above, but using 2 sprigs of sage instead of thyme. Cook 250 g (8 oz) penne until it is just tender, drain and refresh in cold water. Finely slice 250 g (8 oz) bacon and fry until golden, add 10 sage leaves to the pan and fry until crispy. Remove from the pan and drain on kitchen paper. Combine all the ingredients in a large salad bowl, add 100 g (3½ oz) mixed baby salad leaves, 60 g (2¼ oz) feta cheese and season with salt and pepper. Drizzle over olive oil and serve.

balsamic roast vegetable salad

Serves **4**
Preparation time **20 minutes**
Cooking time **30 minutes**

1 **red onion**, roughly chopped
4 **carrots**, roughly chopped
1 **red pepper**, cored,
  deseeded and cut into
  large pieces
1 **sweet potato**, peeled and
  cut into even-sized pieces
400 g (13 oz) **courgettes**,
  peeled and cut into even-
  sized pieces
1 **butternut squash**,
  about 1 kg (2 lb),
  peeled, deseeded and
  cut into chunks
2 tablespoons **olive oil**, plus
  extra to drizzle
150 ml (¼ pint) **balsamic
  vinegar**
1 tablespoon chopped **thyme**
1 tablespoon chopped
  rosemary
75 g (3 oz) **rocket**
salt and **pepper**

Put all the vegetables in a roasting tin and coat well with the oil and balsamic vinegar and add the herbs. Season to taste with salt and pepper and roast in a preheated oven, 190°C (375°F), Gas Mark 5, for 30 minutes until they are cooked and slightly crispy.

Remove the vegetables from the oven, allow to cool slightly, then toss with the rocket. Drizzle with olive oil, check the seasoning and serve.

For herb-crusted rack of lamb with vegetable salad, put 100 g (3½ oz) butter, 100 g (3½ oz) breadcrumbs, 2 tablespoons chopped thyme, 2 tablespoons chopped rosemary, 50 g (2 oz) chopped parsley, 2 crushed garlic cloves and 50 g (2 oz) grated Parmesan cheese into a food processor or blender. Season to taste with salt and pepper and whiz to make a smooth paste. Remove the spiced butter from the food processor, place it between 2 pieces of greaseproof paper and roll it out to 5 mm (¼ inch) thick. Put the butter in the refrigerator to chill. Heat 1 tablespoon vegetable oil in a large frying pan over a high heat and seal 2 x 4-point racks of lamb until golden. Cook the lamb in a preheated oven, 190°C (375°C), Gas Mark 5, for about 12 minutes or until just cooked through. Remove the lamb from the oven and cut a piece of butter to fit over each rack. Cook both racks under a preheated hot grill until golden. Leave to rest for 5 minutes, then slice and serve with the vegetable salad as above.

smoked salmon & potato salad

Serves **4**

Preparation time **15 minutes**

Cooking time **20 minutes**

600 g (1¼ lb) **new potatoes**

2 tablespoons small **capers**

3 tablespoons **Mayonnaise** (see page 12)

2 tablespoons **lemon juice**

1 teaspoon grated **horseradish**

150 g (5 oz) **smoked salmon**

punnet of **mustard** and **cress**, trimmed

salt and **pepper**

Put the potatoes in a saucepan of lightly salted cold water, bring to the boil and cook for 15–20 minutes or until just cooked through. Drain the potatoes and let them cool slightly.

Meanwhile, chop the capers and combine them with the mayonnaise, lemon juice and horseradish. Season to taste with salt and pepper. Put the warm potatoes in a large salad bowl, add the mayonnaise dressing and stir to combine thoroughly.

Arrange the salmon on 4 plates, top with the potatoes and garnish with mustard and cress.

For roast beef & wholegrain mustard potato salad, seal a 450 g (14½ oz) piece of eye fillet until golden, then cook in a preheated oven, 180°C (350°F), Gas Mark 4, for 15 minutes until cooked to medium rare. Remove, cover with foil and allow to rest. Mix 50 ml (2 fl oz) mayonnaise, 2 tablespoons wholegrain mustard, 1 teaspoon Dijon mustard and 5 finely sliced spring onions. Mix through 600 g (1¼ lb) cooked new potatoes and combine well. Thinly slice the beef and serve with the mustard potato salad.

asparagus & rocket salad

Serves **4**
Preparation time **15 minutes**
Cooking time about **5 minutes**

3 tablespoons **olive oil**
   (optional)
500 g (1 lb) **asparagus**
125 ml (4 fl oz) **Tarragon
   & Lemon Dressing** (see
   page 14)
125 g (4 oz) **rocket** or other
   salad leaves
2 **spring onions**, finely sliced
4 **radishes**, finely sliced
salt and **pepper**

To garnish
herbs, such as **tarragon,
   parsley, chervil** and **dill**,
   roughly chopped
thin strips of **lemon rind**

Heat the oil (if used) in a large, nonstick frying pan and add the asparagus in a single layer. Cook for about 5 minutes, turning occasionally. The asparagus should be tender when pierced with the tip of a sharp knife and lightly patched with brown. Remove from the pan to a shallow dish and sprinkle with salt and pepper. Cover with the tarragon and lemon dressing, toss gently and leave to stand for 5 minutes.

Arrange the rocket on a serving plate. Sprinkle the spring onions and radishes over the rocket. Arrange the asparagus in a pile in the centre of the rocket. Garnish with herbs and lemon rind. Serve the salad on its own with bread or as an accompaniment to a main dish.

For grilled asparagus with streaky bacon, remove the woody ends from a large bunch of asparagus, about 500 g (1 lb). Individually wrap the asparagus spears in pieces of streaky bacon, making sure that the bacon covers the base of each spear. Arrange the asparagus in a single layer on a baking sheet and place under a preheated hot grill for 5–7 minutes, turning occasionally until golden and cooked through. Serve the asparagus with the rocket salad as above and drizzle over the tarragon and lemon dressing.

grilled vegetable & haloumi salad

Serves **4**
Preparation time **15 minutes**
Cooking time **25 minutes**

12 **cherry tomatoes on the vine**
4 **portobello mushrooms**
olive oil
2 **courgettes**
500 g (1 lb) **asparagus**
250 g (8 oz) **haloumi cheese**
salt and **pepper**

Dressing
2 tablespoons **olive oil**
2 tablespoons **balsamic vinegar**

Put the tomatoes and mushrooms in a roasting tin, drizzle with about 2 tablespoons oil, season to taste with salt and pepper and cook in a preheated oven, 180°C (350°F), Gas Mark 4, for 10 minutes.

Meanwhile, cut the courgettes into batons about 4 x 2 cm (1½ x ¾ inch) and put them in a large bowl with the trimmed asparagus. Drizzle with olive oil and a pinch of salt and pepper. Heat a griddle pan over a high heat and grill the asparagus and courgettes. Transfer the asparagus and courgettes to the oven with the other vegetables and cook for a further 6–8 minutes.

Cut the haloumi into 5 mm (¼ inch) slices. Heat 1 teaspoon olive oil in a large frying pan over a medium heat and cook the cheese slices until golden.

Make the dressing by whisking the oil and vinegar. Stack the vegetables on serving plates, top with slices of cheese, spoon over the dressing and serve.

For watermelon & haloumi cheese, cut 250 g (8 oz) haloumi into thin slices. Heat 1 tablespoon olive oil in a large, nonstick frying pan and cook the cheese until golden and crispy. Drain and pat dry with kitchen paper. Peel and deseed half a small watermelon and cut it into small triangles. Toss the melon with a small bunch of chopped mint and the diced flesh of 1 ripe avocado. Serve with the grilled haloumi.

roast mushroom salad

Serves **2**
Preparation time **10 minutes**
Cooking time **20 minutes**

2 **portobello mushrooms**,
   each about 150 g (5 oz)
3 tablespoons **olive oil**
1 tablespoon **balsamic**
   vinegar
60 g (2¼ oz) large
   breadcrumbs
3 sprigs of **thyme**, chopped
20 g (¾ oz) **mixed rocket,**
   watercress and spinach
   leaves
salt and **pepper**

Dressing
100 g (3½ oz) **soft goats'**
   cheese
2 tablespoons **olive oil**
2 tablespoons **milk**

Put the mushrooms in a roasting tin and drizzle over 1 tablespoon of the olive oil and the balsamic vinegar. Cook in a preheated oven, 180°C (350°F), Gas Mark 4, for 20 minutes.

Meanwhile, spread the breadcrumbs on a baking sheet with the thyme leaves. Pour over the remaining oil and season with salt and pepper. Place in the oven and cook for 6–8 minutes until golden and crispy.

Make the dressing. Put the cheese, oil and milk in a small saucepan and whisk over a gentle heat until the mixture reaches a pouring consistency, adding a little more milk if it is too thick.

Transfer the mushrooms to serving plates and top with the breadcrumbs. Arrange a handful of the mixed leaves to the side and drizzle with the warm dressing. Serve immediately.

For roast mushroom & prosciutto salad, place 4 slices of prosciutto on a baking sheet and cook in a preheated oven, 180°C (350°F), Gas Mark 4, for 4–5 minutes until crispy. Prepare the mushrooms and breadcrumbs as above and serve the crispy prosciutto with the mushrooms and salad leaves.

squid, fennel & potato salad

Serves **4**
Preparation time **15 minutes,**
  plus cooling
Cooking time **30 minutes**

250 g (8 oz) **new potatoes**
2 **fennel bulbs**
3 tablespoons **olive oil**
500 g (1 lb) prepared **squid**
100 g (3½ oz) **watercress,**
  separated into leaves
salt and **pepper**

Dressing
1 **shallot**, finely chopped
1 red **chilli**, deseeded and
  chopped
rind and **juice** of 1 **lemon**
1 tablespoon chopped **capers**
1 tablespoon chopped **mint**
2 tablespoons **olive oil**

Put the potatoes in a saucepan of lightly salted cold water, bring to the boil and cook for 15–20 minutes or until just cooked through. Drain the potatoes and leave them to cool.

Reserving the fronds for garnish, cut the fennel into thin wedges, leaving the root end intact to hold the pieces together. Put the fennel in a baking tin, drizzle with 1 tablespoon of the oil, season with salt and pepper and cook in a preheated oven, 190°C (375°F), Gas Mark 5, for 15 minutes until roasted and golden.

Meanwhile, cut the potatoes in half. Heat 1 tablespoon of the oil in a frying pan and fry the potatoes until they are crisp and golden. Drain on kitchen paper and transfer to a large salad bowl.

Make the dressing. Mix all the ingredients in a bowl.

Heat the remaining oil in a large frying pan until it is smoking and carefully fry the squid for 2–3 minutes. Add the squid to the bowl. Remove the fennel from the oven, leave to cool slightly and add to the bowl with the dressing and combine gently. Stir through the watercress and serve at once.

For chilli squid salad, mix together 5 tablespoons plain flour, 1 tablespoon chilli powder and 1 teaspoon salt. Dust 500 g (1 lb) prepared squid pieces in the seasoned flour and deep-fry in hot oil for 2 minutes until golden and crunchy. Serve with sliced chilli, fresh coriander and mint leaves, sliced spring onions and lime wedges.

warm tea-smoked salmon salad

Serves **4**
Preparation time **15 minutes**,
 plus resting
Cooking time **10 minutes**

4 **salmon fillets**, each about
 125 g (4 oz)
125 g (4 oz) **cherry
 tomatoes**, halved
125 g (4 oz) **rocket**

Smoke mix
8 tablespoons **jasmine tea
 leaves**
8 tablespoons **soft brown
 sugar**
8 tablespoons **long-grain rice**

Dressing
1 **shallot**, finely chopped
1 **garlic clove**, finely chopped
thyme leaves
1 teaspoon **Dijon mustard**
2 teaspoons **white wine
 vinegar**
4–5 tablespoons **olive oil**
salt and **pepper**

Mix together all the ingredients for the smoke mix. Line a wok with a large sheet of foil, allowing it to overhang the edges, and pour in the smoke mix. Place a trivet over the top. Cover with a tight-fitting lid and heat for 5 minutes or until the mixture is smoking.

Meanwhile, remove any bones from the salmon with tweezers. Put the tomatoes and rocket in a bowl.

Quickly remove the lid from the wok and place the salmon fillets, skin side down, on the trivet. Cover and cook over a high heat for 5 minutes. Remove from the heat and set aside, covered, for another 3 minutes.

Meanwhile, make the dressing. Mix the shallot and garlic in a bowl with the thyme leaves, mustard, vinegar, oil and salt and pepper. Whisk thoroughly to combine.

Flake the salmon into the tomato and rocket salad, add the dressing and toss well. Serve immediately.

For tea-smoked salmon with buckwheat noodle salad, prepare the salmon as above and set aside. Boil 150 g (5 oz) buckwheat noodles for 3 minutes or until just tender. Strain and refresh in cold water, then stir in 1 tablespoon sesame oil and the rind and juice of 1 lime. Add a little more oil if the noodles are sticking together. Mix 100 ml (3½ fl oz) white vinegar, 25 ml (1 fl oz) water and 3 tablespoons caster sugar and stir over a gentle heat until the sugar has dissolved. Allow to cool completely. Finely slice ½ cucumber, add to the cool liquid and infuse for 1 hour. Remove the cucumber from the pickle, mix with the noodles and 125 g (4 oz) rocket and serve with the salmon.

chorizo & quails' egg salad

Serves **4**
Preparation time **15 minutes**
Cooking time **15–20 minutes**

3 tablespoons **olive oil**
200 g (7 oz) medium-hot
  chorizo sausage
1 small **red onion**, cut into
  wedges
1 **garlic clove**, chopped
1 teaspoon **smoked paprika**
1 teaspoon **dried oregano**
8–12 **quails' eggs**
300 g (10 oz) **baby spinach
  leaves**
1 tablespoon **aged sherry
  vinegar**
1 tablespoon **salted capers**
  or **capers in brine**
2 tablespoons chopped
  chives

Heat 1 tablespoon of the oil in a large frying pan over a moderately high heat. Thickly slice the chorizo and fry for about 3 minutes until crisp and golden.

Add the onion and garlic to the frying pan and continue cooking for 2 minutes until the onion is wilted and coloured but not completely soft. Stir in the paprika and oregano and remove from the heat.

Bring a small pan of water to a gentle simmering point. Crack a quail's egg into a small saucer, then drop it carefully into the simmering water. Leave for 1 minute, then remove with a slotted spoon and place on kitchen paper. Keep the egg warm while you poach the remaining eggs.

Wash and dry the spinach leaves and stir them quickly into the chorizo mixture with the remaining olive oil and the sherry vinegar. Arrange on serving plates, scatter with rinsed and drained capers and top each one with 2–3 quails' eggs. Sprinkle the eggs with the chives and serve immediately.

For spinach, chorizo & lentil salad, cook 200 g (7 oz) Puy lentils according to the instructions on the packet, flavouring the water with 1 red chilli sliced lengthways, 2 crushed garlic cloves and 1 teaspoon cumin. Drain the lentils and keep them warm. Prepare the salad as above, mix the lentils through the other ingredients, dress with 1 tablespoon each sherry vinegar and olive oil and serve topped with poached quail eggs.

rice, beans, grains & pasta

sushi rice salad

Serves **2–3**

Preparation time **20 minutes, plus cooling**

Cooking time **30 minutes**

250 g (8 oz) **sushi rice**

6 tablespoons **rice wine vinegar**

2½ tablespoons **caster sugar**

5 g (¼ oz) **pickled ginger,** chopped

½ teaspoon **wasabi**

½ **cucumber**

1 **avocado**, about 175 g (6 oz), peeled and cut into small cubes

250 g (8 oz) **skinless salmon**, cut into bite-sized pieces

8 **spring onions**, finely sliced

To garnish

3 tablespoons **toasted sesame seeds**

Cook the rice according to instructions on the packet.

Meanwhile, put the vinegar and sugar in a small saucepan and heat gently, stirring, until the sugar has dissolved. Turn off the heat and add the chopped pickled ginger and wasabi. Leave to cool. Cut the cucumber in half lengthways and scoop out the seeds with a teaspoon. Slice the flesh finely and add to the cooled vinegar mix.

When the rice is cooked transfer it to a dish, strain the vinegar mixture over it, reserving the cucumber, stir and leave to cool.

Transfer the cooled rice to a large salad bowl and combine gently with the cucumber, salmon, avocado and spring onions. Top with toasted sesame seeds and serve.

For seared tuna & rice salad, mix 2 tablespoons soy sauce with ¼ teaspoon wasabi and brush 300 g (10 oz) tuna loin with the mixture. Roll the tuna in sesame seeds until coated all over. Heat 1 tablespoon vegetable oil in a large frying pan over a high heat and fry the tuna for 1–2 minutes on each side. Remove the tuna from the heat and allow to rest. Prepare the salad as above but omit the salmon. Thinly slice the tuna and serve with the sushi rice salad.

warm orzo salad

Serves **4**
Preparation time **15 minutes,
plus resting**
Cooking time **12 minutes**

250 g (8 oz) **orzo** or
  malloreddus pasta
250 g (8 oz) frozen **peas**,
  thawed
6 tablespoons **olive oil**
6 **spring onions**, roughly
  chopped
2 **garlic cloves**, crushed
8 **marinated artichoke
  hearts**, thinly sliced
4 tablespoons chopped **mint
rind** and **juice** of ½ **lemon
salt** and **pepper**
grated **lemon rind**, to garnish

Cook the pasta in a saucepan of lightly salted boiling
water for about 6 minutes or according to the
instructions on the packet. Add the thawed peas and
cook for a further 2–3 minutes until the peas and
pasta are cooked. Drain well.

Meanwhile, heat 2 tablespoons oil in a frying pan and
stir-fry the spring onions and garlic for 1–2 minutes
until softened.

Stir the spring onions and garlic into the pasta with
the artichokes, mint and the remaining oil. Toss well,
season with salt and pepper, then leave to rest for
10 minutes. Stir in the lemon juice and serve the salad
warm, garnished with lemon rind.

For warm pasta salad with lemony chicken, either
ask your butcher to butterfly a chicken, about 1.25 kg
(2½ lb), for you or do it yourself by cutting down the
backbone without cutting through the breast and
pressing down on the chicken to flatten it. Mix
3 tablespoons olive oil, 2 tablespoons chopped mint,
2 tablespoons chopped parsley, the rind and juice of
1 lemon and salt and pepper. Rub the mixture over the
chicken and allow to marinate for at least 1 hour. Place
the chicken, skin side up, in a foil-lined baking tin and
cook in a preheated oven, 180°C (350°F), Gas Mark
4, for about 40 minutes until cooked though. Allow the
chicken to rest for 5 minutes, then cut it into bite-sized
pieces, arrange them on top of the pasta salad as
above and serve with lemon wedges.

crab & orzo salad

Serves **4**
Preparation time **15 minutes**
Cooking time **20 minutes**

100 g (3½ oz) **orzo pasta**
400 g (13 oz) white cooked
  crab meat
200 g (7 oz) **cherry tomatoes**
125 g (4 oz) **rocket**
rind and **juice** of 1 **lemon**
2 tablespoons chopped
  parsley
1 teaspoon small **capers**,
  rinsed
2 tablespoons **olive oil**

Chilli mayonnaise
200 ml (7 fl oz) **Mayonnaise**
  (see page 12)
1 marinated **red pepper**
1 long **red chilli**, roughly
  chopped
1 teaspoon **lemon juice**
salt and **pepper**

Cook the orzo in a large pan of boiling water according to the instructions on the packet. Refresh and reserve.

Make the chilli mayonnaise. Put the mayonnaise, red pepper and red chilli in a food processor or blender and whiz until smooth. Season to taste with salt and pepper and lemon juice.

Combine the crab and orzo in a large salad bowl. Halve the tomatoes and add them to the bowl with the rocket, lemon rind, parsley and capers and mix carefully. Add 2 tablespoons lemon juice and the oil. Season with salt and pepper and serve with a dollop of the chilli mayonnaise.

For herby mayonnaise, to serve as an alternative with the above salad, chop a mixture of herbs, including chives, chervil, dill, parsley and mint, to make 4 tablespoons. Mix the chopped herbs with 200 ml (7 fl oz) mayonnaise, the rind of 1 lemon and 1 tablespoon lemon juice. Adjust the seasoning with salt and pepper and serve on top of the salad.

lentil & feta salad

Serves **2–4**
Preparation time **15 minutes**
Cooking time **30 minutes**

250 g (8 oz) **Puy lentils**
2 **carrots**, finely diced
2 **celery sticks**, finely diced
100 g (3½ oz) **feta cheese**
2 tablespoons chopped
  parsley

Dressing
3 tablespoons **white wine
  vinegar**
2 teaspoons **Dijon mustard**
5 tablespoons **olive oil**
salt and **pepper**

Put the lentils in a saucepan, cover with cold water and add a pinch of salt. Bring to the boil and cook for 20–25 minutes until just cooked but not mushy. Drain and refresh in cold water, then drain again and transfer to a large salad bowl.

Add the carrots and celery to the bowl with the lentils. Crumble in the feta and add the chopped parsley.

Make the dressing by whisking the vinegar, mustard and oil. Add the dressing to the salad and stir to combine well. Season to taste with salt and pepper and serve immediately.

For lentil salad with poached egg & asparagus,

prepare the lentils as above. Blanch about 500 g (1 lb) asparagus, woody ends removed, refresh and reserve. Cook 250 g (8 oz) sliced pancetta under a preheated hot grill until crispy. Slice the pancetta and asparagus into 3 cm (1¼ inch) pieces, add them to the lentils with 2 tablespoons chopped parsley and 5 tablespoons olive oil and season with salt and pepper. Toss carefully to combine and transfer to serving plates. Put a soft-poached egg on each salad and top with 1 tablespoon of hollandaise sauce on top of the egg.

curried couscous salad

Serves **4**
Preparation time **15 minutes**

juice of **1 orange**
2 teaspoons **mild curry paste**
200 g (7 oz) **couscous**
50 g (2 oz) **sultanas**
300 ml (½ pint) boiling **water**
250 g (8 oz) **smoked
mackerel fillets**
1 small **red onion**, finely
chopped
½ **red pepper**, cored,
deseeded and diced
2 **tomatoes**, chopped
small bunch of **coriander**,
roughly chopped
pepper

Put the orange juice and curry paste into a bowl and stir together. Add the couscous, sultanas and a little pepper, then pour in the boiling water and fork together. Leave to stand for 5 minutes.

Meanwhile, peel the skin off the mackerel fillets and break the flesh into large flakes, discarding any bones.

Add the mackerel, onion, red pepper and tomatoes to the couscous and mix together lightly. Sprinkle roughly chopped coriander over the top, spoon on to plates and serve immediately.

For curried couscous salad with lamb cutlets,
mix 4 tablespoons natural yogurt with 1 teaspoon mild curry paste. Marinate 12 lamb cutlets in the mixture. Prepare the couscous salad as above, omitting the mackerel. Heat 2 tablespoons vegetable oil in a large griddle pan over a high heat and grill the lamb for 3 minutes on each side until cooked through. Serve the lamb on the couscous salad, garnished with chopped coriander.

bean, kabanos & pepper salad

Serves **4**

Preparation time **10 minutes, plus cooling**

Cooking time **20 minutes**

3 **red peppers**, halved, cored and deseeded

1 **red chilli**, deseeded

1 tablespoon **olive oil**

1 **onion**, thinly sliced

75 g (3 oz) **kabanos sausage**, thinly sliced

2 x 400 g (13 oz) cans **butter beans** or **flageolet beans**, drained and rinsed

1 tablespoon **balsamic vinegar**

2 tablespoons chopped **coriander**

Put the peppers and chilli, skin side up, on a baking sheet under a hot grill and cook for 10–12 minutes or until the skins are blackened. Transfer them to a plastic bag, fold over the top to seal and leave to cool. Peel off the skins and slice the flesh.

Meanwhile, heat the oil in a large, nonstick frying pan, add the onion and fry for 5–6 minutes until soft. Add the sausage and fry for 1–2 minutes until crisp.

Put the beans in a large salad bowl. Add all the remaining ingredients and mix well. Serve the salad with walnut bread.

For beef kebabs with bean salad, mix together 1 teaspoon dried chilli, 2 tablespoons sweet red pepper paste, 4 tablespoons olive oil, 1 finely sliced onion, 1 teaspoon ground cumin and 1 teaspoon ground coriander. Marinate 400 g (13 oz) diced beef in the mixture for at least 1 hour, then thread the meat on to metal or presoaked wooden skewers, alternating the meat with pieces of onion and green pepper. Cook under a preheated hot grill for 4 minutes on each side until cooked through. Prepare the salad as above, omitting the kabanos sausage, and serve with the beef kebabs.

orecchiette, bacon & broccoli salad

Serves **4**
Preparation time **15 minutes**
Cooking time **20 minutes**

250 g (8 oz) **broccoli**
300 g (10 oz) **orecchiette pasta**
150 g (5 oz) **pancetta**
150 g (5 oz) **cherry tomatoes**

Dressing
4 tablespoons **Mayonnaise**
  (see page 12)
2 tablespoons **single cream**
2½ tablespoons **tomato sauce**
2 teaspoons **Worcestershire sauce**
3 drops **Tabasco sauce**
1 teaspoon **lemon juice**
salt and **pepper**

Separate the broccoli florets and slice the stems.

Meanwhile, bring a large saucepan of lightly salted water to the boil and cook the pasta for 10 minutes or according to the instructions on the packet. Add the broccoli stems to the saucepan and cook for 2 minutes. Add the florets and cook for a further minute. Drain and refresh in cold water. Transfer to a large salad bowl.

Cut the pancetta into matchsticks and dry-fry for 4 minutes until crispy and golden. Drain on kitchen paper and leave to cool before adding to the pasta. Halve the cherry tomatoes and add them to the pasta.

Make the dressing by combining all the ingredients. Season to taste with salt and pepper. Stir the dressing into the pasta and broccoli and serve immediately.

For warm broccoli & chicken salad, cook the pasta and broccoli as above but do not refresh in cold water. Shred 2 poached chicken breasts and stir the meat into the pasta with 150 g (5 oz) halved cherry tomatoes, 3 tablespoons olive oil, 1 sliced red chilli and 60 g (2¼ oz) grated Parmesan cheese. Garnish with extra grated Parmesan and 2 tablespoons each chopped parsley and chopped basil.

sardine & lentil salad

Serves **4**
Preparation time **15 minutes**
Cooking time **3 minutes**

100 g (3½ oz) frozen **peas**
2 x 120 g (3¾ oz) cans
   boneless, skinless **sardines
   in tomato sauce**
410 g (13½ oz) can **green
   lentils**
5 cm (2 inches) **cucumber**
1 small **red onion**
small bunch of **mint**, roughly
   chopped
grated **rind** and **juice** of
   1 **lemon**
1 **cos lettuce**
pepper

Cook the peas in a saucepan of boiling water for
3 minutes. Alternatively, cook them in the microwave
for 1½ minutes on full power.

Flake the sardines into chunks and put them in a large
salad bowl with their sauce. Rinse and drain the lentils,
dice the cucumber and chop the onion. Add the lentils,
peas, cucumber and onion to the sardines. Add the
mint to the salad with the lemon rind and juice and a
little pepper and toss together.

Separate the lettuce into leaves and arrange them
on serving plates. Spoon the sardine salad on top
and serve.

For potato, sardine & lentil salad, crush 200 g
(7 oz) boiled baby potatoes in their skins and put
them in a baking tin with 200 g (7 oz) cherry
tomatoes. Drizzle with olive oil, salt and pepper and
3 sprigs of thyme. Roast in a preheated oven, 190°C
(375°F), Gas Mark 5, until golden and crispy, then
allow to cool till just warm. Meanwhile, mix together
3 tablespoons chopped parsley, 1 crushed garlic
clove, the rind and juice of 1 lemon and 3 tablespoons
olive oil. Fry 4 fresh sardine fillets in a hot frying pan
for 2–3 minutes each side or until done. Mix the
tomatoes and potatoes with 75 g (3 oz) rocket, then
serve with the sardine fillets on top with the herb
dressing drizzled over.

buckwheat & salmon salad

Serves **4**
Preparation time **15 minutes**
Cooking time **20 minutes**

300 g (10 oz) **buckwheat**
250 g (8 oz) **broccoli florets**
250 g (8 oz) **cherry
  tomatoes,** halved
250 g (8 oz) **smoked salmon**
small bunch of **parsley,**
  chopped
4 tablespoons chopped **dill**
salt and **pepper**

Dressing
juice of 1 **lemon**
3 tablespoons **olive oil**

Put the buckwheat in a saucepan, cover with cold water and add a pinch of salt. Bring to the boil and cook for 10–15 minutes until still firm and not mushy. Drain under running cold water and remove the foam that accumulates. Drain again when cool.

Bring a large saucepan of lightly salted water to the boil and blanch the broccoli florets for 2–3 minutes. Refresh in cold water and drain.

Mix the cherry tomatoes with the buckwheat and broccoli in a large salad bowl. Slice the smoked salmon and add it to the bowl with the parsley and half of the dill.

Make the dressing by whisking the lemon juice and oil. Pour the dressing over the salad, mix lightly to combine and season to taste with salt and pepper. Serve immediately, garnished with the remaining dill.

For smoked salmon & spring green salad, blanch and refresh 400 g (13 oz) assorted green vegetables, including sugar snap peas, mangetout, asparagus, green beans and peas. Put the vegetables in a large salad bowl and add 250 g (8 oz) finely sliced smoked salmon, 1 finely diced red onion, 2 tablespoons chopped parsley, 60 g (2¼ oz) watercress and 2 tablespoons olive oil. Season to taste with salt and pepper and mix lightly. In a small bowl make a lemon crème fraîche dressing by whisking together 4 tablespoons crème fraîche, the rind and juice of 1 lemon, 2 tablespoons chopped dill, 2 tablespoons olive oil and salt and pepper. Drizzle the dressing over the salad and serve.

white bean, feta & pepper salad

Serves **4**

Preparation time **15 minutes, plus cooling**

Cooking time **10—15 minutes**

2 **red peppers**, halved, cored and deseeded

4 tablespoons **olive oil**

2 tablespoons **balsamic vinegar** or **red wine vinegar**

3 teaspoons **sun-dried tomato paste**

4 teaspoons **capers**

2 x 410 g (13¼ oz) cans **cannellini beans** or **haricot beans** or **chickpeas**

½ **red onion**, finely chopped

4 **celery sticks**, sliced

125 g (4 oz) **feta cheese**

1 **cos lettuce**

salt and **pepper**

Put the peppers, skin side up, on a foil-lined grill rack. Brush them with a little of the oil and cook under a preheated grill for 10—12 minutes or until they are softened and the skins charred. Put the peppers in a plastic bag, fold over the top to seal and leave to cool.

Meanwhile, make the dressing by mixing the remaining oil with the vinegar, tomato paste and chopped capers. Season to taste with salt and pepper.

Rinse and drain the beans or chickpeas. Stir them into the dressing with the onion and celery.

Peel the skins off the peppers and cut the flesh into strips. Add to the beans and gently toss together. Crumble the feta cheese over the top and serve the salad on a bed of lettuce leaves.

For white bean, feta & chorizo salad, prepare the salad as above. Cut 3 chorizo sausages into slices and fry them in a large, nonstick frying pan over a high heat until crispy and golden. Remove them from the pan and drain on kitchen paper, reserving the oil in the pan. Add 1 finely diced red onion to the pan and cook for 2 minutes over a low heat. Deglaze the pan with 3 tablespoons vinegar. Pour over the salad and toss to combine. Garnish with 125 g (4 oz) crumbled feta and serve immediately.

puy lentil salad & salsa verde

Serves **4**
Preparation time **15 minutes**
Cooking time **45 minutes**

1 teaspoon **olive oil**
1 small **onion**, finely chopped
300 g (10 oz) **Puy lentils**
450 ml (¾ pint) **vegetable stock**
200 g (7 oz) **cherry tomatoes**, chopped
bunch of **spring onions**, finely sliced

Salsa verde

4 tablespoons chopped **mixed herbs**, such as **parsley, coriander** and **chives**
1 tablespoon **capers**, drained
2 **anchovy fillets** (optional)
1 tablespoon **olive oil**
grated **rind** and **juice** of 1 **lime**

Heat the oil in a saucepan, add the onion and fry for 2–3 minutes until it is beginning to soften.

Add the lentils and stock, bring to the boil, then cover and simmer for 30–40 minutes until the lentils are tender and the stock has been absorbed. Add the tomatoes and spring onions to the lentils. Stir well to mix.

Meanwhile, make the salsa by putting the herbs, capers, anchovies (if used), oil and lime rind and juice in a food processor and whizzing for a few seconds until combined but still retaining a little texture.

Drizzle the salsa over the warm lentils and toss together. Serve with toasted chapattis or flat breads.

For lentil salad with lamb koftas, prepare the lentil salad as above, but using a mixture of 3 tablespoons olive oil and 2 tablespoons chopped mint for the dressing. Mix 400 g (13 oz) lamb mince with 1 teaspoon chilli flakes and 1 finely diced red onion. Chop a small bunch of mint and add it to the mixture with 1½ teaspoons ground cumin. Season to taste with salt and pepper. Take a small handful of the mixture and push it on to a metal or presoaked wooden skewer. Repeat until all the mixture is used. Cook the skewers on a barbecue or under a preheated medium grill, turning occasionally, for 6 minutes or until cooked through. Serve the koftas with the lentil salad and a dollop of Greek yogurt.

farfalle, tomato & pesto salad

Serves **4–6**
Preparation time **10 minutes**
Cooking time **20 minutes**

400 g (13 oz) **farfalle pasta**
5 tablespoons **basil pesto**
  (see below)
100 g (3½ oz) **rocket**
120 g **sun-blushed tomatoes**
small handful of **basil leaves**
60 g (2¼ oz) **Parmesan**
  cheese, grated
salt and **pepper**

Cook the pasta in a large saucepan of boiling water for about 10 minutes or according to the instructions on the packet until it is just tender. Refresh under cold water, drain and place in a large salad bowl. Stir in the pesto so that the pasta is well coated and add the rocket.

Drain the tomatoes and add them to the pasta with the basil leaves and 40 g (1½ oz) of the grated Parmesan. Season with salt and pepper, and serve the salad scattered with the remaining Parmesan.

For basil pesto, to serve with the above salad, separate a large bunch of basil and put the leaves in a food processor or blender with 3 tablespoons toasted pine nuts, 1 small chopped garlic clove and 40 g (1½ oz) grated Parmesan cheese. Whiz until just combined then drizzle in 4–5 tablespoons of olive oil to make a smooth paste. Cover the pesto with a layer of olive oil and keep in the refrigerator for up to 7 days.

wild rice & turkey salad

Serves **4**
Preparation time **10 minutes**, plus cooling
Cooking time **30 minutes**

300 g (10 oz) **wild rice**
2 **green apples**, finely sliced
75 g (3 oz) **pecan nuts**
rind and **juice** of 2 **oranges**
60 g (2¼ oz) **cranberries**
3 tablespoons **olive oil**
2 tablespoons chopped **parsley**
4 **turkey fillets**, each about 125 g (4 oz)
salt and **pepper**

Cook the rice according to the instructions on the packet and allow to cool to room temperature.

Mix the apples into the rice with the pecans, the orange rind and juice and the cranberries. Season to taste with salt and pepper.

Mix together the oil and parsley. Cut the turkey fillets into halves or thirds lengthways and cover with this mixture. Heat a frying pan until it is hot but not smoking and cook the turkey for 2 minutes on each side. Slice the turkey, arrange the pieces next to the rice salad and serve immediately.

For sticky citrus pork chops with wild rice salad, whisk the rind and juice of 1 orange, 2 tablespoons orange marmalade, 1 tablespoon soy sauce and 1 tablespoon sweet chilli sauce. Heat a large frying pan over a high heat and seal 4 pork chops, each about 175 g (6 oz), for 2 minutes on each side. Put the chops on a foil-lined baking sheet and cover with the marinade. Cook in a preheated oven, 180°C (350°F), Gas Mark 4, for 10–15 minutes until cooked through. Prepare the salad as above and serve topped with the pork chops.

pasta, crab & rocket salad

Serves **1**

Preparation time **5 minutes,** plus cooling

Cooking time **10 minutes**

50 g (2 oz) **dried pasta**, such as **rigatoni**

grated **rind** and **juice** of ½ **lime**

2 tablespoons **crème fraîche**

85 g (3¼ oz) can **crab meat,** drained

8 **cherry tomatoes,** halved

handful of **rocket**

Cook the pasta according to the instructions on the packet and leave to cool.

Mix together the lime rind and juice, crème fraîche and crab meat in a large bowl. Add the cooled pasta and mix again.

Add the tomatoes to the bowl with the rocket, toss everything together and serve.

For pasta salad with tuna & chilli, cook the pasta as above. Drain 140 g (4½ oz) can tuna and mix through the cooked pasta. Deseed and finely chop 1 red chilli and add to the pasta with the rind and juice of 1 lemon, 2 tablespoons chopped parsley, a handful of rocket leaves and 2 tablespoons olive oil. Season to taste with salt and pepper and serve.

puy lentils, salmon & dill salad

Serves **4**

Preparation time **30 minutes, plus cooking and chilling**

Cooking time **35–40 minutes**

500 g (1 lb) **salmon fillet**
2 tablespoons **dry white wine**
4 **red peppers**, halved and deseeded
175 g (6 oz) **Puy lentils**
large handful of **dill**, chopped
1 bunch of **spring onions**, finely sliced
lemon juice, for squeezing
pepper

Dressing
2 **green chillies**, deseeded and chopped
large handful of **flat leaf parsley**, chopped
large handful of **dill**, chopped
2 **garlic cloves**
1 teaspoon **Dijon mustard**
8 tablespoons **lemon juice**
1 tablespoon **olive oil**

Put the salmon on a sheet of foil and spoon over the wine. Gather up the foil and fold over at the top to seal. Place on a baking sheet and bake in a preheated oven, 200°C (400°F), Gas Mark 6, for 15–20 minutes until cooked. Allow to cool, then flake, cover and chill.

Grill the peppers and peel away the skins following the instructions on page 174. Reserve the pepper juices.

Make the dressing. Whiz the chillies, parsley, dill, garlic, mustard and lemon juice in a food processor until smooth. With the motor running, drizzle in the oil until the mixture is thick.

Put the lentils and in a large saucepan with plenty of water, bring to the boil, then simmer gently for 15–20 minutes until cooked but still firm to the bite. Drain them and place in a bowl with the red peppers and their juice. Add all the dill and most of the spring onions. Season with pepper to taste.

Stir the dressing into the hot lentils and allow to infuse. To serve, top the lentils with the flaked salmon and gently mix through the lentils and dressing. Add a little lemon juice and the remaining spring onions.

For salmon salad & crushed potatoes, boil 400 g (13 oz) new potatoes for 15–20 minutes. Drain and cool slightly, then lightly crush. Mix in 4 tablespoons olive oil, 2 tablespoons small capers, 1 bunch sliced spring onions and salt and pepper. Prepare the salmon as above and flake it through the potatoes. Add a handful of chopped dill and 100 g (3½ oz) watercress. Serve with lemon and olive oil.

bulgar wheat salad

Serves **4–6**
Preparation time **15 minutes**,
   plus soaking

150 g (5 oz) **bulgar wheat**
400 g (13 oz) **cherry**
   tomatoes, diced
6 **spring onions**, finely
   chopped
1 bunch of **parsley**, chopped
small bunch of **mint**, chopped
salt and **pepper**

Dressing
¼ teaspoon **allspice**
¼ teaspoon **cinnamon**
juice of 1 **lemon**
4 tablespoons **olive oil**

Put the bulgar wheat in a bowl and cover with cold water. Leave to stand for at least 1 hour.

Meanwhile, make the dressing by whisking together the allspice, cinnamon, lemon juice and oil.

Strain the bulgar wheat through a fine sieve and leave to stand for 5 minutes, squeezing out as much water as possible. Add the tomatoes, spring onions, parsley and mint to the bulgar wheat. Add the dressing and mix well. Season with salt and pepper to taste. Leaving the salad in the refrigerator for a few hours will intensify the flavours.

For bulgar wheat salad with whole grilled snapper, score the snapper 3 times diagonally on each side. Mix together 1 teaspoon ground cumin, ¼ teaspoon turmeric, 1 teaspoon ground ginger, 1 teaspoon ground chilli, the rind and juice of 1 lemon and 2 tablespoons olive oil. Put lemon slices inside the fish and rub them with the spice mixture. Put the fish under a low grill and cook for 20–25 minutes, turning half way through cooking, until opaque but still juicy. Put the bulgar wheat salad on a large serving plate, arrange the grilled snapper on top and serve.

mushroom & ricotta pasta salad

Serves **4—6**
Preparation time **20 minutes**
Cooking time **12 minutes**

250 g (8 oz) **ricotta cheese**
2 tablespoons chopped
 parsley
2 tablespoons chopped
 rosemary
2 tablespoons chopped
 thyme
2 tablespoons chopped **basil**
75 g (3 oz) **Parmesan
 cheese**, finely grated
400 g (13 oz) **penne pasta**
2 tablespoons **olive oil**
500 g (1 lb) mixed
 mushrooms, including
 chestnut and **portobello**
1 **garlic clove**, crushed
salt and **pepper**

Mix the ricotta with the herbs and Parmesan in a small bowl and season to taste with salt and pepper.

Cook the pasta in a large saucepan of boiling water for 10 minutes or according to the instructions on the packet until it is just tender.

Meanwhile, slice the mushrooms. Heat the oil in a large frying pan over a high heat and fry the mushrooms for 1 minute. Add the crushed garlic, season with salt the pepper and cook for 2 minutes.

Drain the cooked pasta, add the mushrooms and stir through. Add the ricotta mixture and mix well. Serve with more chopped herbs and Parmesan, if liked.

For pancetta & creamy mushroom pasta, cut 200 g (7 oz) pancetta into small batons and fry until crispy. Add to the cooked pasta together with the mushrooms. Stir through 100 g (3½ oz) baby spinach and serve.

corn, tomato & black bean salad

Serves **4**
Preparation time **10 minutes**
Cooking time **10 minutes**

4 **corn cobs**, leaves and fibres
   removed
250 g (8 oz) **cherry
   tomatoes**, halved
400 g (13 oz) can **black
   beans**, drained and rinsed
1 **red onion**, finely diced
1 **avocado**, peeled, stoned
   and diced
small bunch of **coriander**,
   roughly chopped

Dressing
juice of 1 **lime**
2 tablespoons **rapeseed oil**
2–3 drops **Tabasco sauce**

Cook the corn cobs in boiling water for 7–10 minutes.
Cool briefly under running cold water then scrape off
the kernels with a knife. Put the kernels in a large bowl
with the tomatoes, black beans, onion and avocado and
mix with the coriander.

Make the dressing by mixing together the lime juice, oil
and Tabasco.

Drizzle the dressing over the salad, stir carefully to
combine and serve immediately.

For chilli prawns with corn & black bean salad,
finely chop 2 garlic cloves and deseed and finely chop
2 long red chillies. Heat 1½ tablespoons vegetable oil
in a wok or large frying pan over a high heat and cook
24 peeled and butterflied prawns with the tails on.
Stir-fry for 1 minute, then add the garlic and chillies.
Fry for a further 2 minutes until just cooked through.
Turn off the heat and stir through 3 tablespoons
chopped coriander. Serve the prawns over the corn
and black bean salad garnished with extra coriander
leaves and lime wedges.

chickpea & herb salad

Serves **4**
Preparation time **10 minutes,**
 plus cooling
Cooking time **10 minutes**

100 g (3½ oz) **bulgar wheat**
4 tablespoons **olive oil**
1 tablespoon **lemon juice**
2 tablespoons chopped **flat**
 leaf parsley
1 tablespoon chopped **mint**
400 g (13 oz) can **chickpeas,**
 drained and rinsed
125 g (4 oz) **cherry**
 tomatoes, halved
1 tablespoon chopped **mild**
 onion
100 g (3½ oz) **cucumber**
150 g (5 oz) **feta cheese**
salt and **pepper**

Put the bulgar wheat in a heatproof bowl and pour over sufficient boiling water just to cover. Set aside until the water has been absorbed. If you want to give a fluffier finish to the bulgar wheat, transfer it to a steamer and steam for 5 minutes. Spread on a plate to cool.

Mix together the olive oil, lemon juice, parsley and mint in a large salad bowl. Season to taste with salt and pepper. Add the the chickpeas, tomatoes, onion and bulgar wheat.

Dice the cucumber and add to the bowl. Mix well and add the diced feta, stirring lightly to avoid breaking up the cheese. Serve immediately.

For beetroot & chickpea salad, combine 150 g (5 oz) baby chard with 400 g (13 oz) rinsed and drained chickpeas, 200 g (7 oz) precooked and diced beetroots in a large mixing bowl. Cut an orange in half and put the halves on a hot griddle pan until golden and not black. Squeeze the juice into a small bowl and add 1 teaspoon clear honey and 3 tablespoons olive oil. Whisk together, then dress the salad lightly and crumble over 150 g (5 oz) feta.

chickpea & cherry tomato salad

Serves **4**

Preparation time **15 minutes**, plus soaking and cooling

Cooking time **1–1½ hours**

250 g (8 oz) **dried chickpeas**

400 g (13 oz) **cherry tomatoes**, halved

4 **celery sticks**, sliced

4 **spring onions**, sliced

50 g (2 oz) **Kalamata olives**

Mint and **Yogurt Dressing** (see page 15)

black pepper

mint leaves, to garnish

Soak the chickpeas overnight in cold water. Drain the chickpeas, rinse well and drain again. Put them into a large saucepan, cover with plenty of cold water and bring to the boil. Simmer for 1–1½ hours or according to the instructions on the packet until cooked and soft. Add extra water if necessary. Drain and allow to cool.

Put the tomatoes, celery, spring onions, olives and chickpeas into a large serving bowl and mix well. Stir in the dressing, season with black pepper, garnish with mint leaves and serve.

For chickpea salad with harissa lamb, marinate 12 lamb chops in 3 tablespoons harissa paste mixed with 2 tablespoons olive oil. Leave the lamb to marinate for at least 1 hour, preferably overnight. Prepare the chickpea salad as above. Heat a large griddle pan and fry the lamb in batches for 2–3 minutes on each side until just cooked through and still pink in the middle. Remove and allow to rest for 5 minutes. Serve with the salad, drizzled with the Mint & Yogurt Dressing and some roughly chopped mint.

risoni, sweet potato & bacon salad

Serves **4–6**
Preparation time **20 minutes**
Cooking time **30 minutes**

2 large **sweet potatoes**,
    peeled and cut into small
    dice
2 tablespoons **olive oil**, plus
    extra for drizzling
200 g (7 oz) **smoked streaky
    bacon**
250 g (8 oz) **risoni** or **orzo
    pasta**
200 g (7 oz) frozen **peas**
100 g (3½ oz) **feta cheese**
small bunch of **mint**, chopped
salt and **pepper**

Put the sweet potatoes on a large baking sheet
and drizzle with olive oil and salt and pepper. Bake in
a preheated oven, 190°C (375°F), Gas Mark 5, for
20–25 minutes until just cooked through.

Finely slice the bacon. Heat a large frying pan over a
high heat and fry the bacon for 4 minutes until golden
and crispy. Drain on kitchen paper and reserve.

Meanwhile, cook the pasta in a large saucepan of
boiling water for 10 minutes or according to the
instructions on the packet. Add the peas and cook for
2 more minutes and drain.

Remove the sweet potatoes from the oven and mix
with the pasta and peas. Add the bacon and crumble
over the feta, reserving some of both for garnish. Add
2 tablespoons olive oil and the chopped mint and
combine well. Garnish with the reserved bacon and feta
and serve.

For cajun chicken & risoni salad, drizzle 2 boneless,
skinless chicken breasts with olive oil and sprinkle
over 2 tablespoons cajun seasoning. Heat a frying pan
and fry the chicken for 5 minutes on either side until
cooked through. Thinly slice the chicken and serve
with the risoni salad as above.

fruit salads

mixed berry salad

Serves **4–6**
Preparation time **10 minutes**

400 g (13 oz) **strawberries**
250 g (8 oz) **raspberries**
150 g (5 oz) **blueberries**
150 g (5 oz) **blackberries**
small bunch of **mint**, finely
    chopped, a few sprigs
    reserved for decoration
3 tablespoons **elderflower**
    syrup

Hull and halve the strawberries. Wash all the berries and drain well.

Add the chopped mint to the berries with the elderflower syrup, mix carefully and serve, decorated with the reserved mint sprigs.

For warm berry salad, dilute 100 (3½ fl oz) elderflower syrup in 600 ml (1 pint) water, add 50 g (2 oz) caster sugar and bring to the boil in a heavy-based saucepan. Add 400 g (13 oz) strawberries, 250 g (8 oz) raspberries, 150 g (5 oz) blueberries and 150 g (5 oz) blackberries, prepared as above, to the pan and turn off the heat. Let the berries cool slightly, then serve with vanilla ice cream. The berries will keep for up to 5 days in the syrup in the refrigerator.

exotic fruit salad

Serves **6–8**

Preparation time **10 minutes**

1 large ripe **pineapple**, about 1.5 kg (3 lb)

1 **papaya**, about 400 g (13 oz)

3 **passion fruit**

juice of 1 **lime**

mint sprigs, to decorate

Peel and core the pineapple and cut the flesh into small wedges. Do the same with the papaya, carefully removing the seeds with a spoon. Put the pineapple and papaya in a serving bowl.

Cut the passion fruit in half and scrape the pulp into the bowl. Add the lime juice, mix carefully and serve decorated with mint sprigs.

For grilled pineapple with lime sugar, peel a 1.5 g (3 lb) pineapple and cut it into quarters, removing the core. Cut each quarter into 4 long pieces and thread them on to metal or presoaked wooden skewers. Put the rind of 3 limes into a food processor and add 150 g (5 oz) granulated sugar. Whiz briefly then spread the sugar on a baking sheet and leave to dry for at least 1 hour. Heat a griddle pan to a medium heat and cook the pineapple for 2 minutes on each side until golden and caramelized. Sprinkle with the lime sugar and serve. Store unused lime sugar in a dry, airtight container.

citrus salad

Serves **4–6**

Preparation time **15–20 minutes,** plus marinating

Cooking time **5 minutes**

2 **oranges**

2 **satsumas**

2 **limes**

4 **blood oranges**

1 **ruby grapefruit**

150 g (5 oz) **caster sugar**

150 ml (¼ pint) **water**

Remove the rind from the 2 oranges and the 2 limes using a zester. Peel all the fruit with a knife, carefully removing all the pith. Slice the oranges and satsumas and segment the limes, blood oranges and grapefruit.

Reserve some of the orange and lime rind for decoration and put the rest into a saucepan with the sugar and water and cook over a gentle heat, stirring until the sugar has dissolved. Pour the syrup over the fruit and leave to stand in the refrigerator for at least 1 hour before serving. Serve decorated with the reserved orange and lime rind.

For Grand Marnier citrus sauce, to serve with citrus salad, mix 100 g (3½ oz) caster sugar, the juice and rind of 2 oranges and 50 ml (2 fl oz) water in a small, heavy-based saucepan. Bring to the boil, then turn the heat to low and reduce the liquid by two-thirds until syrupy. Once the correct consistency is reached, add 50 ml (2 fl oz) Grand Marnier, pour over the citrus salad and serve.

rhubarb & strawberry salad

Serves **4**
Preparation time **20 minutes**
Cooking time **20 minutes**

500 g (1 lb) **rhubarb**
125 g (4 oz) **caster sugar**
150 ml (¼ pint) **water**
1 **vanilla pod**
2 teaspoons **rosewater**
400 g (13 oz) **strawberries**

To serve
mascarpone cheese or
  Greek yogurt
40 g (1½ oz) roughly chopped
  pistachio nuts

Cut the rhubarb into 4 cm (1½ inch) lengths and put them in a shallow, non-metallic ovenproof dish.

Put the sugar and water in a small saucepan over a low heat and stir until the sugar has dissolved. Add the vanilla pod and rosewater. Pour the syrup over the rhubarb, cover with foil and bake in a preheated oven, 180°C (350°F), Gas Mark 4, for 12–15 minutes until just soft.

Meanwhile, hull and halve the strawberries. When the rhubarb is cooked, discard the vanilla pod and add the strawberries, cover and leave to stand for 5 minutes. Transfer the fruit to serving plates, spoon some of the cooking liquid over each one and add a dollop of mascarpone or yogurt and a sprinkling of chopped pistachios.

For rhubarb, apple & scallop salad, prepare 500 g (1 lb) rhubarb as above but add only 75 g (3 oz) sugar. Cut an apple into matchsticks and combine in a bowl with the rhubarb, 100 g (3½ oz) watercress and 1 sliced avocado. Heat 1 tablespoon vegetable oil in a large frying pan over a high heat and fry 12 large scallops for 2 minutes on each side until just cooked through. Remove and keep warm. Toss the salad with 1 tablespoon white balsamic vinegar, 2 tablespoons olive oil and salt and pepper. Arrange the scallops on top of the salad and serve.

spiced fruit salad

Serves **6**
Preparation time **15 minutes**,
    plus cooling and chilling
Cooking time **2 minutes**

1 **vanilla pod**, plus extra for
    decorating if liked
2½ tablespoons **caster sugar**
175 ml (6 fl oz) **water**
1 **hot red chilli**
4 **clementines**
2 **peaches**
½ **cantaloupe melon**
175 g (6 oz) **blueberries**

Use the tip of a small, sharp knife to score the vanilla pod lengthways through to the centre. Put the sugar and water in a saucepan and heat gently until the sugar dissolves. Halve and deseed the chilli and add it to the saucepan with the vanilla pod. Heat gently for 2 minutes, then remove the pan from the heat and leave the syrup to cool.

Cut away the rind from the clementines and slice the flesh. Remove the stones from the peaches and slice the flesh. Deseed the melon and cut the flesh into small chunks, discarding the skin.

Mix the fruits in a serving dish and pour over the warm syrup, discarding the chilli and vanilla pod. Leave the syrup to cool completely, then cover the fruit salad and chill until you are ready to serve. Decorate with a vanilla pod if liked.

For spiced fruit salad syrup, to serve with the above fruit salad, add to the syrup 1 lemon grass stalk cut in half and bruised with a meat tenderizer, 3 kaffir lime leaves and 2 cm (¾ inch) fresh root ginger peeled and roughly sliced. Add these with the chilli and prepare in the same way.

poached fruit with ginger biscuits

Serves **6–8**
Preparation time **15 minutes**
Cooking time **20 minutes**

250 g (8 oz) **caster sugar**
2.5 litres (4 pints) **water**
1 **vanilla pod**, plus extra for
   decorating if liked
4 **peaches**
4 **nectarines**
10 **apricots**

To serve
mascarpone cheese
3 **ginger biscuits**, crushed

Put the sugar, water and vanilla pod in a large, heavy-based saucepan and heat gently, stirring, until the sugar has dissolved. Bring to a low simmer, add the fruit and cover with a circle of greaseproof or baking parchment to hold the fruit in the syrup. Simmer for 2 minutes then turn off the heat and leave to cool.

Remove the fruit from the liquid with a slotted spoon, reserving the poaching liquid. Peel the skins from the fruit, then cut them in half and remove the stones.

Put 250 ml (8 fl oz) of the poaching liquid in a small, heavy-based saucepan and heat to reduce it for 6–8 minutes until it has a syrupy consistency. Put the fruit in a large bowl, pour over the syrup and toss gently. Arrange the fruit on serving plates, add a spoonful of mascarpone to each one and sprinkle with crushed ginger biscuits. Decorate with a vanilla pod if liked.

For poached stone fruit with raspberry coulis, put 150 g (5 oz) frozen raspberries and 40 g (1½ oz) caster sugar in a heavy-based saucepan. Slowly bring up to the boil, stirring, to dissolve the sugar. Simmer for 2–3 minutes until the coulis has a syrupy consistency. Remove from the heat and strain through a fine sieve. Poach the stone fruit as above and serve with the raspberry coulis and a drizzle of custard.

mixed fruit salad

Serves **6—8**
Preparation time **15 minutes**

¼ **watermelon**
½ **galia melon**
1 **mango**
2 **green apples**
2 **bananas**
3 **kiwifruit**
200 g (7 oz) **strawberries**
150 g (5 oz) **blueberries**

Peel and deseed both the melons and cut the flesh into 2—3 cm (1 inch) chunks. Put them in a large bowl. Peel and dice the mango, dice the apples and slice the bananas. Add to the bowl with the melon.

Peel the kiwifruit and cut the flesh into rounds, add to the bowl along with the berries and mix the fruit together carefully.

For exotic fruit salad with passion fruit cream, whisk together 4 tablespoons mascarpone cheese, 200 ml (7 fl oz) double cream and 2 tablespoons sifted icing sugar in a bowl until soft peaks form. Gently fold in the pulp of 2 passion fruit. Serve a spoonful with the exotic fruit salad.

cherries with cinnamon crumble

Serves **4—6**
Preparation time **15 minutes**,
  plus cooling
Cooking time **20 minutes**

1.5 kg (3 lb) **cherries**, pitted
250 g (8 oz) **caster sugar**
400 ml (14 fl oz) **water**
1 **vanilla pod**
2 **cloves**
strips of **orange peel**, to
  decorate

Crumble
60 g (2¼ oz) **fruit loaf**
15 g (¼ oz) **unsalted butter**
⅛ teaspoon **cinnamon**
1 tablespoon **caster sugar**

Cinnamon cream
1 tablespoon **icing sugar**
150 ml (¼ pint) **whipping
  cream**
¼ teaspoon **cinnamon**

Put the cherries in a large bowl. Place the sugar in a heavy-based saucepan and add the water, vanilla pod, cloves and orange peel. Bring to the boil, stirring occasionally, then pour the syrup over the cherries. Leave to cool.

Make the crumble. Cut the fruit loaf into 1 cm (½ inch) dice. Melt the butter and drizzle it over the fruit loaf. Mix together the cinnamon and sugar and sprinkle over the fruit loaf. Mix well, transfer to a baking sheet and cook in a preheated oven, 190°C (375°F), Gas Mark 5, for 4—5 minutes until golden and crunchy. Remove the crumble from the oven and allow to cool.

Meanwhile, make the cinnamon cream. Sift the icing sugar over the cream, add the cinnamon and whisk until firm peaks form.

Serve the cherries with a small amount of syrup, a spoonful of the cinnamon cream and a sprinkling of the fruit loaf crumble. Decorate with strips of orange peel.

For chocolate & cinnamon sauce, to serve with the cherries, combine 100 g (3½ oz) chopped dark chocolate (use chocolate with 70 per cent cocoa solids), 15 g (½ oz) butter, 125 ml (4 fl oz) cream and ½ teaspoon ground cinnamon in a small, heavy-based saucepan over a low heat. Stir the sauce until all the chocolate has melted and it is smooth and glossy. Turn off the heat and reserve. Prepare the cherries as above and serve with a drizzle of the chocolate cinnamon sauce.

winter fruit salad

Serves **4–6**
Preparation time **5 minutes**
Cooking time **30 minutes**

100 g (3½ oz) **prunes**, stoned
100 g (3½ oz) ready-to-eat
  dried peaches
100 g (3½ oz) ready-to-eat
  dried pears
100 g (3½ oz) ready-to-eat
  dried apples
100 g (3½ oz) ready-to-eat
  dried apricots
50 g (2 oz) ready-to-eat **dried
  figs**
1 **cinnamon stick**
4 **cloves**
rind of 1 **lemon**
50 g (2 oz) **caster sugar**

To serve
Greek yogurt
clear honey

Put the prunes and the ready-to-eat dried fruits, the cinnamon stick, cloves, lemon rind and sugar in a saucepan and cover with cold water. Set over a medium heat and simmer for 15 minutes until the fruit plumps up.

Remove the pan from the heat and strain the fruits, reserving the liquid and discarding the cinnamon stick. Return the liquid to the heat for 10 minutes until reduced.

Return the fruits to the syrup, warm them through and serve with some yogurt and a drizzle of honey.

For roast winter fruit salad, core and quarter 3 pears and 3 apples and put them in an ovenproof dish. Halve and stone 3 plums and add them to the dish with 50 g (2 oz) dried figs, 50 g (2 oz) frozen cranberries, a cinnamon stick and 4 cloves. Dot the fruit with 50 g (2 oz) unsalted butter, then sprinkle with 50 g (2 oz) soft brown sugar. Bake in a preheated oven, 180°C (350°F), Gas Mark 4, for 20 minutes until soft. Serve with Greek yogurt and honey.

fruit salad with lemon grass syrup

Serves **4–6**
Preparation time **10 minutes**,
    plus cooling
Cooking time **10 minutes**

1 cm (½ inch) **fresh root
    ginger**, peeled and sliced
1 **lemon grass stalk**, lightly
    bruised
100 g (3½ oz) **caster sugar**
150 ml (¼ pint) **water**
2 **papaya**, peeled and
    deseeded
2 **mangoes**, peeled and
    stoned
2 **guavas**, peeled and stoned
10 **lychees**, peeled
2 tablespoons **toasted
    coconut**

Put the ginger, lemon grass, sugar and water into
a small, heavy-based saucepan and simmer for
5 minutes. Remove from the heat and allow to cool.

Cut the papaya flesh into long wedges and put them
in a bowl. Cut the mangoes and guavas into small
wedges and add to the papaya with the lychees. Add
3 tablespoons of the syrup and combine carefully.

Transfer the salad to serving dishes, drizzle over
some of the remaining syrup and sprinkle with the
toasted coconut.

For toasted coconut, to decorate the fruit salad,
break open a coconut, drain away the juice and peel
off the outer tough husk. Run a vegetable peeler along
the broken edge of the coconut. Once you have
enough shavings, lay them flat on a baking sheet and
toast in a preheated oven, 200°C (400°F), Gas Mark
6, for 3–4 minutes until golden brown.

chargrilled fruit with chilli salt

Serves **6—8**
Preparation time **15 minutes**
Cooking time **10 minutes**

1 large **mango**, peeled and stoned
½ **pineapple**, peeled
2 **bananas**
½ teaspoon **crushed dried chilli**
1 tablespoon **sea salt** or **vanilla sea salt**

Cut the mango into 2 cm (¾ inch) pieces and cut the pineapple into small wedges. Cut the bananas into thick slices. Skewer the fruit on to metal or presoaked wooden skewers, alternating the fruits.

Mix together the chilli and salt and set aside.

Preheat a griddle pan to medium heat and grill the skewers on each side for 3 minutes until golden and caramelized. Remove the skewers from the heat, sprinkle with the salt chilli mix and serve.

For vanilla sea salt, to accompany chargrilled fruit skewers, scrape the seeds of 1 vanilla pod into a small bowl with 4 tablespoons sea salt. Stir to combine well and leave to infuse for at least 2 hours.

papaya, lime & almond salad

Serves **4**
Preparation time **15 minutes**,
plus cooling
Cooking time **3–5 minutes**

3 firm, ripe **papayas**, peeled
and deseeded
2 **limes**
2 teaspoons **light brown
sugar**
50 g (2 oz) **toasted blanched
almonds**
lime wedges, to decorate

Cut the papayas into large dice.

Finely grate the rind of both limes, then squeeze
1 of the limes and reserve the juice. Cut the pith off
the second lime and segment the flesh over the bowl
of diced papaya to catch the juice. Add the lime
segments and grated rind to the papaya.

Pour the lime juice into a small saucepan with the
sugar and heat gently until the sugar has dissolved.
Remove from the heat and leave to cool.

Pour the cooled lime juice over the fruit and toss
thoroughly. Add the toasted almonds and serve with
lime wedges.

For papaya & lime salad with ginger granite, pour
1 litre (1¾ pints) ginger beer into a rectangular plastic
container. Mix in 3 tablespoons chopped mint, put the
container in the freezer and leave for at least 4 hours.
When the liquid is frozen scrape it with a fork until a
fluffy ice has formed. Spoon the ice over the papaya
and lime salad and serve immediately.

marsala poached pears

Serves **6**

Preparation time **10 minutes**

Cooking time **40 minutes**

300 ml (½ pint) **Marsala**

500 ml (17 fl oz) **red wine**

200 g (7 oz) **caster sugar**

2 tablespoons **lemon juice**

1 **cinnamon stick**

2 **star anise**

6 **pears**

clotted cream, to serve

Put the Marsala, red wine, sugar, lemon juice, the cinnamon stick and star anise in a heavy-based saucepan and bring to a low simmer.

Peel the pears, leaving the stalks in place, put them in the saucepan and cook for 20–25 minutes, turning occasionally, until they are soft. Remove the pears from the saucepan with a slotted spoon and set aside to cool.

Meanwhile, return the poaching liquor to the heat and boil to reduce for about 10 minutes until it is thick and syrupy. Serve the pears, drizzled with the syrup and accompanied by a spoonful of clotted cream.

For roasted pears with toffee sauce, halve 6 pears and remove the stones. Put the pears in an ovenproof dish and sprinkle with 5 tablespoons brown sugar and 1 teaspoon vanilla extract. Dot with 20 g (¾ oz) unsalted butter. Roast the pears in a preheated oven, 180°C (350°F), Gas Mark 4, for 20 minutes until golden and soft. Meanwhile, combine 150 g (5 oz) brown sugar, 125 ml (4 fl oz) cream and 20 g (¾ oz) unsalted butter in a heavy-based saucepan, stirring until the sugar has dissolved. Simmer for 2 minutes then pour the sauce over the roasted pears and serve with a dollop of clotted cream.

melon & pineapple salad

Serves **4**

Preparation time **10 minutes**, plus standing

½ **cantaloupe melon**, peeled and deseeded
½ small **pineapple**, peeled
grated **rind** of 1 **lime**
2 teaspoons **fructose**
lime slices, to decorate

Dice the melon and pineapple. Add the melon and pineapple to a bowl or plastic container.

Mix together the lime rind and fructose until well combined. Sprinkle this over the fruit and stir in well; in an hour or so the fructose will have dissolved. Decorate with the lime slices and serve.

For lime & ginger syrup, to serve with the above salad, in a small, heavy-based saucepan combine 150 g (5 oz) caster sugar, 150 ml (¼ pint) water, the rind and juice 1 lime and 1 cm (½ inch) fresh root ginger, peeled and roughly sliced. Bring the mixture to the boil, stirring occasionally to dissolve the sugar. When the sugar has completely dissolved, remove the syrup from the heat, cover and chill. Drizzle the syrup over the salad about 30 minutes before serving to allow the flavours to combine.

index

acknowledgements

Executive Editor: Nicola Hill
Senior Editor: Charlotte Macey
Executive Art Editor: Leigh Jones
Designer: Jo Tapper
Photographer: Lis Parsons
Home Economist: Sunil Vijayaker
Props Stylist: Liz Hippisley
Production Controller: Marián Sumega

Special photography: © Octopus Publishing Group Limited/Lis Parsons.
Other photography: © Octopus Publishing Group Limited 55, 79, 101, 121, 139, 161, 173, 175, 179, 183, 185, 201, 231, 234; /Jeremy Hopley 39, 51; /Dave Jordan 159; /William Lingwood 59, 63, 89, 93, 96, 117, 127, 167, 203; /Peter Myers 45; /William Reavell 193; /Gareth Sambridge 151, 191, 217; /Phillip Webb 105.